Drama and Creative Activities for Young Children

Janet Rubin and Margaret Merrion

Humanics Learning
P.O. Box 7400
Atlanta, GA 30357

Design and Illustrations by Susan Chamberlain

PRINTED IN THE UNITED STATES OF AMERICA

Library of Congress Cataloging-in-Publication Data

Rubin, Janet.
    Drama and music: creative activities of young children/by Janet Rubin and Margaret Merrion .
       p. cm.
    Includes bibliographical references.
    ISBN 0-89334-236-X
    1. Drama in education.   2. Music in education.   I. Rubin, Janet.
    II. Title.
PN3171.M48 1995
371.3'32 – dc20   94-24087
                                             CIP
                                             AC

DEDICATION
To our sisters

ACKNOWLEDGEMENTS

Kathy Fehrman
Shirley Friedland
Frances Kadas
David Nelson
Saun Strobel

Drama & Music: Creative Activities for Young Children

Table of Contents

APPENDICES

Introduction

We wrote *Drama and Music: Creative Activities for Young Children* for teachers who recognize that youngsters have creative potential just waiting to be tapped. Expertise in conducting these activities isn't as necessary as a genuine desire to bring out the expressive abilities of young children and to have an enjoyable learning experience. This book contains a fund of activities which are designed to foster children's native capacity to be creative. This book also provides the schemata for teachers to stretch their creative potential. Teachers will learn to design original creative exercises individually tailored for their instructional styles and student needs.

We present the activities in a progressive order unfolded with increasing complexity. Name games, finger plays, and nursery rhymes serve as excellent foundational experiences for more complex creative exercises involving instruments, stories, pantomime, and choral reading. The continuum of creative ability, however, varies markedly within each individual and classroom. Our experience has affirmed that designating age-appropriateness or recommending grade level is not a precise process. Children learn at different rates and possess skill/ability levels that vary from school to school. Rather, we respect the teacher's judgment in determining the appropriateness of any given exercise. The teacher works closest with the children and can schedule activities at the most propitious time developmentally.

We recommend that teachers approach the activities in this book with a spirit of adventure and yet with a sense of structure. Help maintain a creative environment by allowing divergent thinking, fostering imaginative responses and asking open-ended questions. Maintain structure by mentally rehearsing the activity and planning its execution. We also urge teachers to collaborate in the creative enterprise. Collaboration involves laboring together, exploring one's creative and expressive self and the group's collective reservoir of creativity.

Finally, whether the exploration involves pantomime, movement, or song, teachers, as collaborators, will enjoy the creative process and serve as powerful models in the classroom. With such collaboration, amazing results are bound to occur.

We wish you twofold success – in these creative experiences with your children and in your development as a creative teacher.

Unleashing Your Creative Potential

We are pleased to share with you some of our best practices in using creative drama and music in the classroom. All of these techniques have been used many times over with children and teachers. In fact, many times our audiences will suggest more creative variations for these activities. We gratefully acknowledge these recommendations. We hope you, too, will trust your creative self and adapt them accordingly.

This book is organized with the following structure in mind; *Part One:* Unleashing Your Creative Potential, *Part Two:* Activities, Activities, Activities, *Part Three:* Furthering Your Creative Potential. Appendices are provided for further recommendations to help enhance children's creativity.

PART ONE: UNLEASHING YOUR CREATIVE POTENTIAL

We hope to introduce you to the types of activities found in the body of the book and to provide some teaching suggestions to assure success.

The activities are presented in a deliberate order. They are intended to work with K-3 children, i.e., kindergarten through grade three. Some of the activities are applicable for more than one age group; others are more simple or sophisticated – narrowing their application to a more select age group. We acknowledge that you are the best person to assess the capabilities of your children. You may, for example, have an advanced, gifted group of first graders. We would hope that you would use the activities that seem most suitable, skipping some of the early "openers." On the other hand, your students may have had little or no experience with creative drama or music. In that case, do not hesitate to look to the beginning activities which meet your childrens' needs, interests and abilities. You can build up to the appropriate level as the school year progresses.

We introduce you to almost thirty different types of activities throughout the book. We have tried to package them in an easy-to-read, practical-to-use format with straight-forward vocabulary. Many times we point out exactly what you should ask or discuss with the class. You, of course, are the best judge of the most appropriate vocabulary and language. We also recognize that the learning characteristics of children are diverse and trust that you will be sensitive to the individual differences of your students. Please consider our suggestions as only recommendations.

Within each activity category, there is a subtle order to the activities. Name games, for example, progress from simple and general to complex and specific. Though the activities are not necessarily prerequisites for one another, you will find that subsequent activities are sometimes linked to or emanate from earlier ones. In both creative drama and music activities, skill building is encouraged and richer artistic products result from increased competence. Please note the ordering of activities in this progression.

Finally, we have examined national curricular guides to ascertain broad concepts and skills which find their way into most core subject areas, such as science, health, mathematics, and language arts. It will be apparent that, in addition to exploring creative drama and music, children can acquire other content knowledge or skills. The purpose of this collection is to expand children's creative potential through creative drama and music. It is possible, nonetheless, for by-product learning in other subject areas to take place.

In order to facilitate successful creative drama and music experiences we would like to introduce concepts designed to help you and the children to have rewarding and productive creative efforts.

Control

To an observer, it sometimes appears that when children are engaged in musical and creative drama activities, discipline has been greatly relaxed or is not being applied. This should not be the case. The challenge for the teacher is to construct an environment in which the children feel comfortable expressing themselves in creative ways and yet to maintain a climate that is respectful and safe for all children. Control is the term applied to establishing and maintaining this type of classroom environment.

A control word or device should be introduced to the children at the start of the lesson and then used whenever the children's behavior merits it. If possible, incorporate imaginative techniques for classroom maintenance into activities. You might, for example, tell the children during a safety lesson that when they hear you say, "Red light!" they are to stand perfectly still. Some common mechanisms for control include the use of the terms "freeze," and "stop." Some teachers flick the lights in the classroom, use a sound meter made of cardboard with an arrow to indicate when the noise level in the room has become too loud, or simply raise their hand or put their finger to their lips when children need to tone down their behavior.

We urge you to present and use control positively. It is difficult to ask children for creative responses if they feel that they are too strictly regulated. If, however, a child's behavior is disruptive and attempts to channel it more constructively have not worked, ask the child to step out of the action for awhile. Be certain to let him or her know that it is the behavior and not the person that displeases and that he or she is welcome to again participate in activities whenever his or her actions are more acceptable. Let your students know that you want them to enjoy participating and disruptive actions make this difficult for all.

Voice and Body in Creative Drama

In dramatic work, the two most obvious and important means available to the participant for self-expression are voice and body. Actors train these instruments diligently for theatrical careers. While we do not expect young people to become professional performers, we have included exercises in this book which tune these instruments in an age appropriate fashion.

In creating a character, and in all of the activities which lead toward that goal, being able to speak clearly, expressively, and with adequate projection (dynamics) contributes to development of a vocal range which serves children in all types of oral communication. Likewise, being physically in control and knowing how to manipulate the body to achieve diverse characterizations brings adeptness in sending and interpreting non-verbal messages.

Young children often seem to be less self-conscious than adults when it comes to engaging in vocal and physical exercises. Their freedom of expression should be valued and enjoyed.

Replay and Evaluation

In creative drama, replay is the repetition of an activity for the purpose of improving the quality of the effort, including new ideas, or giving new children a turn. Replay should always have a positive purpose and should not be used to call undue attention to poor performance. An activity can be replayed as many times as the children or you desire, as long as interest and improvement are in evidence.

Replay goes hand in hand with evaluation which is an assessment of how the children have just played an activity, scene, or story. Evaluation is most effective when students comment and the teacher guides the discussion. Students should start evaluative comments with positive remarks and move from there to noting areas for improvement. Along with their criticisms, they should be able to say why they liked or disliked something or why it did or did not work. Help the children to identify *why* they feel as they do, going beyond simply saying they liked something or it was not good. When appropriate, guide them to evaluate by character name rather than by classmates' names, as this keeps them thinking about characterization and avoids putting players on the spot. A repeated pattern of evaluation and replay is common in dramatic activities and often necessary if children are to move beyond superficial interpretation or effort.

Sidecoaching

In creative drama, sidecoaching is used to help deepen involvement in an activity. It is the descriptive comments or questions spoken by the teacher to help children move beyond superficial play. Two key ideas should be remembered about sidecoaching. First, your questions and comments are rhetorical. No answers should be given nor expected. Second, sidecoaching comments are not simply repeated directions. Notice the difference in the following statements.

What color is your balloon? What shape is it? How do you feel as you watch it float away? (sidecoaching)

Be sure to leave space between you and your neighbor as you imagine your balloon floating in the sky. (direction)

Sidecoaching comments can be made aloud to the whole class or given quietly to an individual who may be having difficulty with a particular exercise. In the latter instance, simply stand next to the person and sidecoach quietly. If your sidecoaching has been effective, you should see the results in the child's improved interpretation.

Preview Play

In some activities or with certain children, you may feel that you'd like to see some of their ideas before they show their work to classmates. In these instances, request that the children engage in preview play. The term means that you are asking the children to give you a sneak peak of their ideas. This allows you to see where they are headed in an exercise and to assist them if the choices seem inappropriate. Rough play, nonsensical interpretations, and so forth are usually readily apparent in preview play and children can then be guided to produce more satisfying results.

Knowledge of Music

We have assumed the teacher has a rudimentary knowledge of music. A simple guide to reading rhythmic notation and using an elementary vocabulary follows. Since the vocabulary should be used by the children, please become familiar with it first.

PART TWO: ACTIVITIES, ACTIVITIES, ACTIVITIES

This bountiful collection of activities is a warehouse of creative experiences teachers can use for brief lessons or as extended lessons. The activities are designed to "stand alone," that is, they can be complete experiences in themselves. It is also possible, however, to link activities together, as suggested in the text.

We urge teachers to rehearse the activity in their minds before implementation, anticipating classroom management decisions which may support the lesson, such as grouping children, distributing and collecting instruments, providing signals for beginning and closing performances, and so forth. The rehearsal will also serve as practice in pacing and timing the flow of the lesson.

Another consideration is the actual placement of the lesson within the school day. Care should be given to selecting the most propitious time to engage children in these high-interest activities.

PART THREE: FURTHERING YOUR CREATIVE POTENTIAL

We conclude the book with suggestions for extending the activities and researching further resources to enhance creative lessons. We believe teachers have the innate ability to design activities after the models contained in the book. These recommendations will guide the pursuit of creative teaching. The activities are laid out in 4"x 6" card format for easy filing. Two other sources for creativity enhancement are *The Reading Resource Book* and *Storybook Classrooms*, both published by Humanics Learning.

HOW TO READ MUSICAL NOTATION

We have assumed that the teacher has rudimentary knowledge of music. This is to say, we do not expect teachers to read music fluently, yet many teachers have some familiarity with basic concepts. The songs reprinted within this book use traditional notation, as they are intended for the teacher's eyes only.

The rhythmic exercises, however, use a system of basic notation that is easy for the teacher to acquire and is appropriate for children to learn at the primary level. We suggest you review the symbols used in the system and practice them within familiar musical contexts. The rhythmic notation system involves using only the stems of traditional notation. For example, in standard notation, the quarter note has a note head and stem. In this rhythmic system, we shall be working with stem notation. See the conversion chart below.

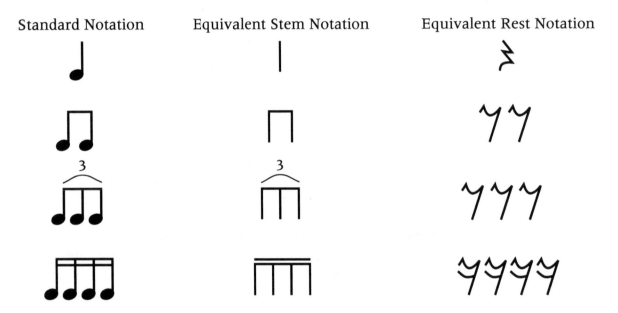

Standard Notation	Equivalent Stem Notation	Equivalent Rest Notation

VOCABULARY

Some teachers may have used vocabulary words to represent rhythms. Words, such as "walk," "run-ning," and "gal-lop-ing," have been used to represent rhythms, stressing syllabication for quarter, eighth, or triplet figures. We find that youngsters are able to learn the notation and vocabulary used in this book more effectively if it is used consistently in the classroom. This is a system which is often used and recognized by music teachers in other settings. Therefore, consistent usage will contribute to reinforcement of musical literacy.

The simple rhythmic vocabulary is based on syllables that represent note lengths. The system on the following page illustrates the basic beat value and its subdivisions.

Notation Symbols with Vocabulary

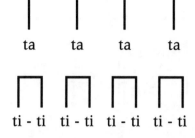

ta   ta   ta   ta

ti - ti   ti - ti   ti - ti   ti - ti

ti-ri - ti-ri ti-ri - ti-ri ti-ri - ti-ri ti-ri - ti-ri

ta   ti   ta   ti

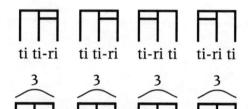

ti ti-ri   ti ti-ri   ti-ri ti   ti-ri ti

tri-o-la tri-o-la tri-o-la tri-o-la

OTHER SYMBOLS

Similar to standard notation, a vertical line separates rhythms into bars or measures. A double bar line indicates the end of the rhythmic material.

A meter number will be given at the outset of the rhythm. This number signifies how many beats each measure contains. For example:

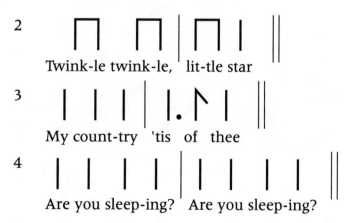

2   Twink-le twink-le, lit-tle star

3   My count-try 'tis of thee

4   Are you sleep-ing? Are you sleep-ing?

Unleashing Creative Potential

9

A repeat sign involves two dots before the double bar line. This typically occurs at the end of a section of the song or at the song's end. A slur is a short curved line connecting two notes together rhythmically. The first of the tied notes is performed and held the combined value of the notes tied together.

Activities,
Activities, Activities

NAME GAMES

Name games are useful methods of providing an anticipatory set, motivating children to actively participate in the activities which follow, and establishing a creative classroom environment. Getting to know each other and feeling comfortable with peers are important steps in establishing a warm and artistically conducive climate. Name games are a simple way for the children to become acquainted and to launch creative play.

A number of the name games can involve making name tags and serve to introduce the topic or theme of the lesson. Even after the children know one another, the name tag gives them a point of identification which will be useful in the subsequent activities. Sometimes it is practical for you to make part or all of the name tag. Other times, we hope that the construction of the name tag is another creative experience for the children. Be resourceful in the use of materials here. Wall paper, burlap, paper plates, and other items can be used innovatively.

Try the following name games in the early days of the school year. Even after the children know each other, consider returning to these for the enjoyment they provide.

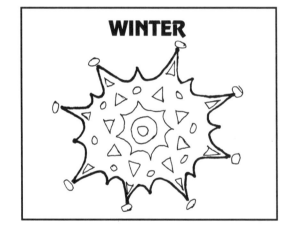

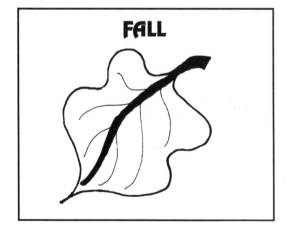

1. NAMES ARE FUN

Names are fun
Names are fun
Let's learn names of everyone.
(Each child now says his or her name, keeping a beat within the chant, i.e., Mary, Michael, Lamar, Sarajini. Now, repeat the chant with the following change.)

Names are fun
Names are fun
I know the names of everyone.
(In unison, the children now repeat everyone's names.)

2. MY FAVORITE THINGS

Seat the children in a circle and instruct each child to say his or her name and favorite thing to do at school. *Ex.* My name is Jayna and I like to write on the chalkboard. Try some of the following variations.

- favorite thing to do on weekends
- favorite thing to eat
- favorite animal
- favorite place to visit
- favorite game or sport

3. WHO ARE YOU?

Going around the circle, speak the first, second, and fourth lines of the chant in unison. The third line is spoken by each child when it is his or her turn.

Who are you?
Who are you?
I am *(child's name)*.
How do you do?

4. BODY PARTS

Make name tags in the shape of body parts such as eyes, ears, lips, feet, and hearts. Allow children to color their name tag.

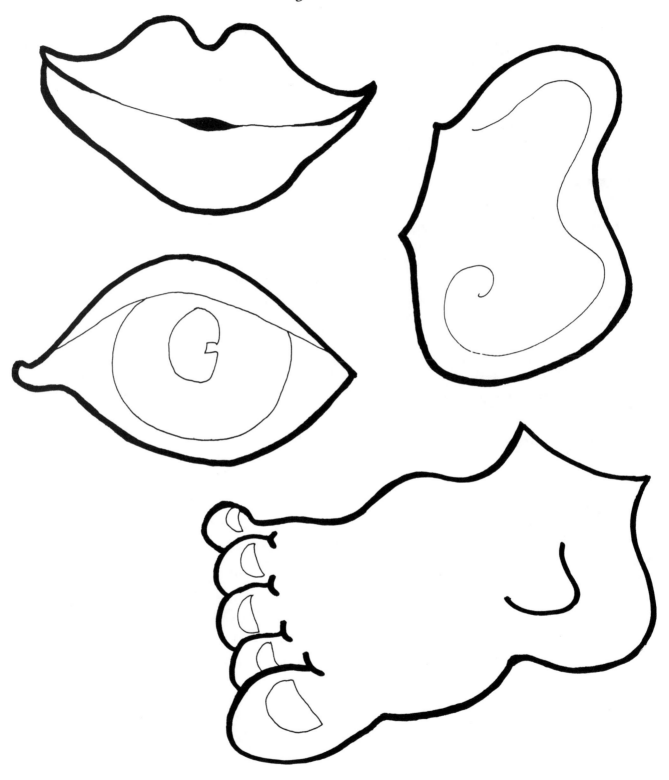

Drama & Music: Creative Activities for Young Children

5. HEAD AND SHOULDERS

Learn the song *Head and Shoulders*. After singing the African-American game song, substitute body parts which appear on the children's name tags. Invite the children to point to the respective body part as it is sung. Form a circle and sing the song again with the new body terms. Have the children take one step toward the center when the body term on their name tag is mentioned in the song.

The children will be able to grasp the song, including all of the verses and new lyrics, due to the great amount of repetition in the words and music. Songs which have such a high degree of repetition are useful for drill in learning body parts. This song lends itself to reinforcing terms for other content, too. Days of the week, for example, can be reviewed in sequential order.

"Sunday, Monday, baby, one, two, three,
Tuesday, Wednesday, baby, one, two, three,
Thursday, Friday, Saturday, Sunday, baby, one, two, three."

Can you think of other facts you would like to review to the music of *Head and Shoulders*?

 ADDITIONAL IDEA

• The song Looby Loo would be a fun way for children to learn body parts. See page 155 for music.

HEAD AND SHOULDERS

1. Head - shoul - ders, Ba - by, one, two, three; Head -
2. Shoulders - chest, Ba - by, one, two, three; Shoulders-
3. Chest - knees, Ba - by, one, two, three; Chest -

shoul - ders, Ba - by, one, two, three; Head - shoul - ders, head —
chest, Ba - by, one, two, three; Shoulders - chest, shoulders -
knees, Ba - by, one, two, three; Chest - knees, chest —

Coda:

shoul - ders, Head - shoul - ders, Ba - by, one, two, three.
chest, Shoulders - chest, Ba - by, one, two, three.
knees, Chest - knees, Ba - by, one, two, three.

I ain't been to 'Fris - co, And I ain't been to school; I

(Spoken:)

ain't been to col - lege, but I ain't no fool. To the front, to the back, to the

(Spoken:)

front, to the back, to the si - si side,___ to the si - si side.___

Use both hands to touch the body parts, in the rhythm of the song.

4. Knees – ankles, Baby, …	7. Chest – shoulders, Baby, …
5. Ankle – knees, Baby, …	8. Shoulders - head, Baby, …
6. Knees – chest, Baby, …	Coda

6. COLORS

To the tune of *Johnny Get Your Haircut, Mary Wore a Red Dress* is another simple song with a good deal of repetition. It simply goes,

Mary wore a red dress, red dress, red dress;
Mary wore a red dress, all day long.

The name tags can be of any type for this activity. The point is to learn the children's names while reinforcing color recognition. After the song is learned, begin variations by naming a color of a particular clothing item each child has worn to class. For example, "Shanda wore a blue skirt, blue skirt, blue skirt; Shanda wore a blue skirt, all day long." "Ya'akov wore a brown belt...."

For additional fun, bring to class scarves, hats, boots and gloves of various colors. Allow the children to select an item of clothing for more colorful variations.

7. THE SOLAR SYSTEM

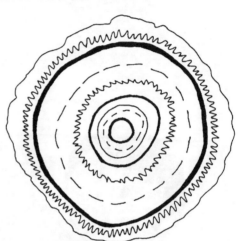

Have the children select one of the nine planets and paint a picture of it to wear as a large name tag. Encourage the children to paint or size their planet according to identifiable characteristics, such as rings, clouds, colors, etc. Cut the planets out and wear them.

Tape nine circles around a center "sun" on the gym or classroom floor. Select nine children to be the planets, or have two or more children play each of the planets if you wish to involve all of the children. Each "planet" should orbit one of these circles. Play new age music and have the children move as they think their planet does (quickly, slowly, etc.) around the sun. If you wish, a child can be selected to portray the sun.

To further expand upon the study of the planets, select two children to be futuristic "astro-journalists" who have the ability to make the planets talk. Have these children interview each planet. Children being interviewed should respond in character, i.e., "I am Mars. I am known as the red planet."

8. SAFETY NAME GAME

This name game gets the children thinking about good health habits and safety. With the youngsters sitting in a circle, ask each to say his or her name and something that he or she can do to stay healthy and safe. Some word in the child's statement must start with the same letter as the first letter of his or her name.

Ex.   My name is Demetrius and I can exercise daily.
        My name is Maureen and I won't play with matches.
        My name is Yoko and I will eat yellow and green vegetables.

FINGER PLAYS

Finger plays are especially well suited for kindergarten children, although they are enjoyed by children throughout early childhood. They are simple, engage the imagination, and incorporate movements which are within the physical capabilities of the young child. We suggest demonstrating the actions and familiarizing the children with the words before putting speech and movement together. Children will frequently want to repeat those finger plays that they have mastered and particularly enjoy.

Use finger plays as a springboard for discussing all sorts of current topics and curricular concepts including safety, conduct with strangers, animal care, and the difference between fantasy and truth.

Drama & Music: Creative Activities for Young Children

1. FIVE LITTLE MONKEYS

Five Little Monkeys is a fun way to reinforce subtraction facts in math. In this finger play, help children feel the beat of the lyrics while illustrating the events of the rhyme:

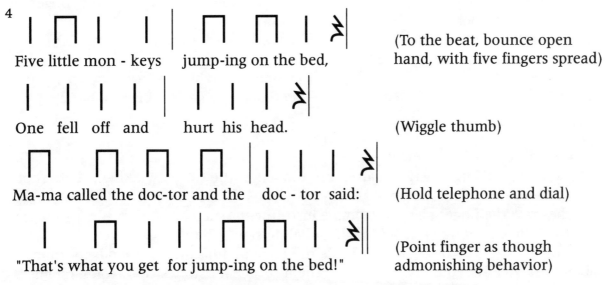

Five little mon - keys jump-ing on the bed,   (To the beat, bounce open hand, with five fingers spread)

One fell off and   hurt his head.   (Wiggle thumb)

Ma-ma called the doc-tor and the   doc - tor said: (Hold telephone and dial)

"That's what you get for jump-ing on the bed!"   (Point finger as though admonishing behavior)

Second verse: Begin with four fingers and lose one for each subsequent verse. Continue through fourth verse.

Fifth verse: One little monkey jumping on the bed.
                   She fell off and hurt her head....

Final verse: No little monkeys jumping on the bed.
(show zero with fingers):   None fell off nor hurt their heads.
                                Mama loved the monkeys and the monkeys said:
                                "We learned a lesson 'bout jumping on the bed!"

2. CABIN IN THE WOOD

In a cabin in the wood,   (Show peaked roof with both hands)
Little old man at the window stood,   (Imitate looking through binoculars with hands on forehead)

Saw a rabbit hopping by,   (Signify rabbit hopping with two fingers)
Knocking at the door.   (Knock)
"Help me! Help me! Sir," he cried,   (Raise hands for each "help me" cry)
"Before a hungry fox catches me."
"Little rabbit, come inside,   (Motion for rabbit to come towards you)
Safely to abide."   (Pet rabbit by smoothing one hand)

 ADDITIONAL IDEAS

• Pantomime the finger play. Children can dramatize the story by taking the parts of the old man, rabbit and the fox.
• Orchestrate the finger play with simple instruments, such as rhythm sticks to represent the knocking sound and a triangle or bell to signal the call for help.
• Read A.A. Milne's stories about Winnie the Pooh and his animal friends for more rabbit tales. Beatrix Potter is another excellent source for stories concerning rabbits.

3. BEEHIVE

Here's the beehive   (Make fist with right hand and place on left palm)

Where are the bees?   (Look inside fist)
Hiding behind where nobody sees.   (Place hands behind back)
Watch and you'll see them come out of the hive: (Make fist and look inside)
One-two-three-four-five!   (Count with fingers)
ZZZZZZZZZZZ   (Make fingers fly away)

 ADDITIONAL IDEA

• Change the number of bees to ten so that both hands may be involved in the finger play during the counting.

4. TWO LITTLE BLACK BIRDS

Two little black birds sitting on a hill	(Hands behind back)
One named Jack, one named Jill.	(Bring one index finger forward for each bird)
Fly away Jack, fly away Jill.	(Move each index finger behind back for each bird)
Come back Jack, come back Jill.	(Bring index fingers forward again for each bird)

5. NIGHT AND DAY

Now it's night	(Start with hand raised, fingers form an "o" for the moon)
and time for bed.	(Lower hand and pull back covers)
On my pillow rests my head.	(Rest head on hands as if sleeping)
Now it's day	(Form "o" for sun with fingers; raise hand)
and I arise.	(Stretch and yawn)
Wipe the sleep out of my eyes.	(Rub eyes)

6. TOSS THE BALL

Toss the ball	(Tossing motion)
Toss the ball	(Tossing motion)
Toss the ball so high	(Tossing motion and look up)
Catch the ball	(Catching motion)
Catch the ball	(Catching motion)
Falling from the sky	(Cup hands and look at them)

7. THE TALL FINE PINES

The tall fine pines In my front yard	(Stand up straight)
Stately, swaying	(Sway side to side)
Standing guard	(Stand at attention)
Bowing, bending	(Bend at the waist)
In the breeze	(Turn from waist in a circular motion)
Wind can't break These mighty trees	(Flex muscles)

Activities, Activities, Activities

8. EIGHT O'CLOCK

Eight o'clock, eight o'clock	(Hold up eight fingers)
Time for bed	(Fold hands and rest head on them)
Nine o'clock, ten o'clock	(Hold up nine and then ten fingers)
Sleepy head	(Yawn)
'Round the face of my clock	(Hold both hands up, then have right hand make a circle around the left, like the hand of a clock)
Hands do go	
Seconds, minutes, hours	(Repeat moving like the hand of the clock)
Time does grow	
Six o'clock, seven o'clock	(Hold up six and then seven fingers)
Slept all night	(Stretch arms and yawn)
Eight o'clock, eight o'clock	(Hold up eight fingers)
Morning light	(Shield eyes as if looking at the sun)

9. MONSTERS EVERYWHERE

Monsters short,	(Lower hand)
Monsters tall,	(Raise hand)
Scary,	(Gnash teeth)
Friendly,	(Smile)
And that's not all!	
Some are happy,	(Smile)
Some are sad.	(Pretend to cry)
Some are angry,	(Angry face)
Some are bad.	(Wag finger)
But we like monsters	(Place hand on heart)
here and there.	(Point left then right)
We like monsters	
everywhere!	(Spread arms)

Drama & Music: Creative Activities for Young Children

NURSERY RHYMES AND CHANTS

We hope you will be generous in introducing children to the wealth of rhymes and chants that are part of our cultural history. We have, by virtue of space limitations, only included a few of these. There is a warehouse collection in your library. Reviewing them will bring back fond memories.

We recommend that you start each day with a rhyme. Rehearse it periodically and, before ending the school day, ask the children to recite it by themselves so that they can share it with their families on their own. Review previously learned rhymes daily so that students build a repertory.

The activities which are suggested with the select rhymes in this book can be applied to others easily. Also, the rhymes themselves will form a body of literature which can be used creatively in other dramatic and musical settings. You will be pleasantly surprised at how much children derive from memorizing, pantomiming, and reflecting upon rhymes and chants.

Activities, Activities, Activities

1. TEDDY BEAR

This old jump rope chant is a favorite with young children. The words suggest specific movements.

Teddy bear, Teddy bear, turn around,
Teddy bear, Teddy bear, touch the ground,
Teddy bear, Teddy bear, show your shoe,
Teddy bear, Teddy bear, that will do.
Teddy bear, Teddy bear, go up stairs,
Teddy bear, Teddy bear, say your prayers,
Teddy bear, Teddy bear, say good night,
Teddy bear, Teddy bear, turn out the light.

 ADDITIONAL IDEA

• Notice that each line of the rhyme (except the final line) has the rhythm:

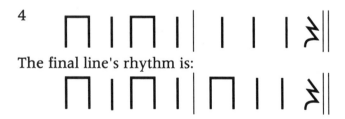

The final line's rhythm is:

After the children know the rhythm of the rhyme very well, assign individual children to play the rhythm of each line on a different instrument, with all instruments joining in for the final line.

2. PAT-A-CAKE

Pat-a-cake, pat-a-cake, baker's man.
Roll it and roll it as fast as you can.
Pat it and prick it and mark it with a "B."
Put it in the oven for Baby and me.

💡 ADDITIONAL IDEAS

• Invite children to substitute a different letter for their favorite doll, toy, baby sister or brother. The result will change the last two lines to "...mark it with a "J." Put it in the oven for Jason and me."

• Notice that the rhythm of the first line is exactly the same as the Teddy bear rhyme:

4 ⊓ ⊓ ∣ ∣ ∣ ∣ 𝄾 ‖

• Have the children be your echo and clap the rhythm of each line of the rhyme after you.

Line 1: ⊓ ⊓ ∣ ∣ ∣ ∣ 𝄾 :‖

Line 2: ⊓ ∣ ⊓ ∣ ⊓ ∣ ∣ 𝄾 :‖

Line 3: ⊓ ∣ ⊓ ∣ ⊓ ⊓ 𝄾 :‖

Line 4: ⊓⊓⊓ ∣ ⊓ ∣ ∣ 𝄾 :‖

Activities, Activities, Activities

• For a completely different rhythmic experience, sing this version of the rhyme.

3. HICKORY DICKORY DOCK

Hickory, dickory, dock.
The mouse ran up the clock.
The clock struck one,
The mouse ran down.
Hickory, dickory, dock.

 ADDITIONAL IDEAS

• Keep the beat of the clock by providing an "ostinato," (a persistent underlying pattern) of "tick, tock, tick, tock..." Ask a few children to chant softly the ostinato while others recite the rhyme. Begin with eight "tick, tock" patterns, then cue in the rhyme. Allow the "tick, tock" ostinato to continue for eight patterns after the chant is finished.
• Transfer the "tick, tock" sound to rhythm sticks. Play a triangle when the clock strikes "one."
• Supply actions for the rhyme: Line 1: Swing arm for pendulum motion.
　　　　　　　　　　　　　　　　　Line 2: Walk fingers upward.
　　　　　　　　　　　　　　　　　Line 3: Clap once.
　　　　　　　　　　　　　　　　　Line 4: Walk fingers downward.
　　　　　　　　　　　　　　　　　Line 5: Swing arm for pendulum motion.
• Discuss different sizes of clocks. According to the size, vary the movements of an index finger (for watches), hands/forearms (for medium size clocks), and whole arms (for the pendulum of grandfather clocks).
• Substitute different times within the chant. Using a classroom clock as a model, show the children two o'clock. In the rhyme, create new words to fit the time change. For example, "The clock struck two, the mouse said 'boo'..."
• Play different instruments to the rhythm of each line of the rhyme.

Activities, Activities, Activities

27

4. HEY, DIDDLE DIDDLE

Recite the following rhyme with a decided beat, emphasizing the underlined words or syllables. Notice how most of the important figures in this rhyme are stressed on the beat. Help the children feel the stresses by patting their thighs (patschen).

Hey, diddle, diddle, the cat and the fiddle,
The cow jumped over the moon.
The little dog laughed to see such sport,
And the dish ran away with the spoon.

 ADDITIONAL IDEAS

• Sometimes nonsense nursery rhymes are the best sources for creative interpretation. After all, children can be naturally nonsensical! Ask the children to interpret the movements of the cat, fiddle, cow, moon, little dog, dish and spoon with straw puppets.

Cut out small figures of each character/item in the chant and staple them to the top of a straw (see patterns on following page). Ask the children to move their puppets creatively to the "hey diddle, diddle" portion. Experiment with different ways the puppet can show laughter and running away.

• Follow this rhyme with songs about animals mentioned in *Hey Diddle Diddle*, such as *Had Me a Cat*, *Old MacDonald*, or *Bingo*.

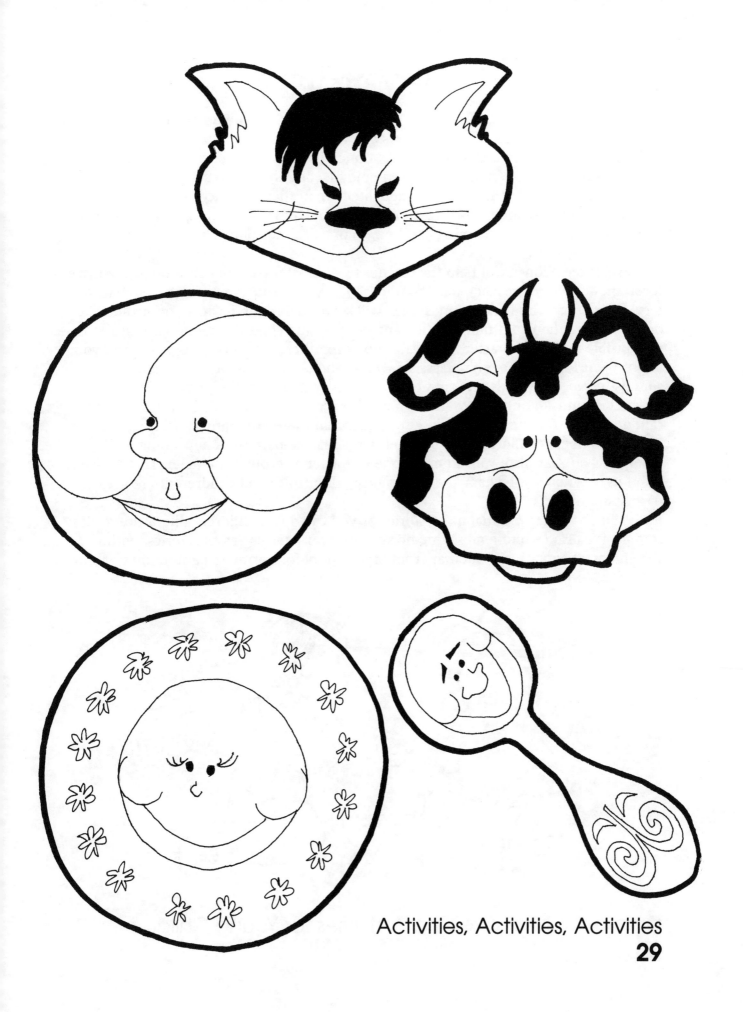

Activities, Activities, Activities

29

NOISY STORIES

Noisy stories are a delightful way to engage the children in verbal participation. Stories are constructed so that characters are assigned a sound, word, phrase, or sentence and whenever that character is mentioned in the story, the children loudly make the appropriate response. Children enjoy feeling that the teacher needs their help in telling the story and they are delighted when they are encouraged to say the character's sound as loudly as they can without, of course, screaming or yelling. It is especially important, with young children, to practice the sounds before telling the story.

Several techniques will help the teacher to successfully lead noisy stories. First, we recommend that the teacher star (*), underline, **bold**, or in some way mark characters in the story who make sounds. This will serve as a reminder to stop for the children's contributions. Further, you'll want to group the children so that each group is responsible for one character. Be aware, however, that with very young children you might want to have the entire class, as well as the teacher, do all of the character sounds in unison. We also recommend that the teacher limit the number of characters assigned sounds to only a few and to have those characters appear frequently and in random order. Children tend to lose interest when there are many characters making limited numbers of appearances or when a predictable pattern of appearances emerges. You may also want to make one character a "group" character. This device is often used when some characters have fairly minor roles and children desire greater participation.

It's fun to create original noisy stories or you can adapt children's literature to this format. We also recommend saving noisy stories for later use as the stories, without the character sounds, are often appropriate material for narrative pantomimes or story dramatizations.

Drama & Music: Creative Activities for Young Children

1. A DRIVE THROUGH SHAPESVILLE

Rectangle - two long and two short   Circle - round and round
Triangle - three points   Car - vroom
(It is recommended that the car be a group sound in this noisy story.)

It is a beautiful Sunday afternoon and Mr. **Rectangle** and his two friends, Ms. **Circle** and Mr. **Triangle** decide to go for a drive through Shapesville. They all get into Mr. **Rectangle's car**, buckle their seat belts, and Mr. **Rectangle** slowly backs the **car** out of the driveway, looks both ways to be certain there is no traffic, and pulls the **car** onto the street. They drive to the corner, where Mr. **Rectangle** stops for the stop sign. "This is my favorite traffic sign," says Ms. **Circle**. "The "O" in S-T-O-P looks like me."

Continuing on their way, Mr. **Rectangle** comes to a one way street. "Turn here," says Mr. **Triangle**. Mr. **Rectangle** turns the car onto the street and says to his friends, "The sign for this street has two long sides and two short sides. It looks like me."

"My favorite sign is at this corner," says Mr. **Triangle** as the **car** approaches the intersection of Union and Main Streets. "It is a yield sign and it has three sides like me."

As the **car** travels along Main Street, the friends see a sign for the Shapesville Elementary School. "The school sign has two **triangles** put together," says Mr. **Triangle**. "One points up and the other points down."

"Let's drive our **car** across the railroad tracks on our way home," requests Ms. **Circle**. "The sign for the railroad crossing is a **circle** with an X inside."

Mr. **Rectangle** smiles at his friends, Ms. **Circle** and Mr. **Triangle**. "It is fun to take a drive through Shapesville," he says. "There are so many **circles**, **triangles**, and **rectangles** to see."

Activities, Activities, Activities

2. KAYLA'S PRESENT

Kayla - What time is it?
Alarm Clock - Beep, beep, beep
Cuckoo Clock - Cuckoo, cuckoo

Mom - Happy birthday, dear
Grandfather Clock - Bong, bong
Wristwatch - Tick, tock

Kayla's alarm clock rings and she reaches over to hit the snooze button. In a few minutes, the **alarm clock** rings again. **Kayla** slowly opens her eyes. "Today is my birthday!" she remembers. "I hope I get a **wristwatch** as a present." **Kayla** quickly runs to the kitchen where **Mom** is fixing breakfast. "**Mom**," asks **Kayla**," when is my party?" "When you hear the **cuckoo clock** in the den, it will be time for your party. Until then, get dressed and watch television."

Kayla runs back to her room and looks at her **alarm clock**. Her **alarm clock** also has a radio and she plays it as she gets dressed. "I don't want to miss hearing the **cuckoo clock**," **Kayla** thinks aloud and she shuts off her radio. "I'll watch television in the family room."

The **grandfather clock** stands in a corner of the family room and **Kayla** looks as the pendulum swings back and forth. "I can count the times the **grandfather clock** chimes whenever I want to know the time," says **Kayla** to herself, "but it makes a loud noise. I don't like to stand too close to the **grandfather clock**. Sometimes the **grandfather clock** scares me." **Kayla** turns on the television in the family room but, before long, she becomes impatient and goes back to the kitchen. "What time is it, **Mom**?" asks **Kayla**. Just then, **Kayla** hears the **cuckoo clock** announce the time.

"**Kayla**," says **Mom**, "I want to give you a special present." She puts a brightly wrapped box in **Kayla's** hand. **Kayla** unwraps the box to find a **wristwatch**. "It is just what I wanted!" **Kayla** exclaims. "I will learn to tell time and now, when I look at my **wristwatch**, I will always know the minutes and the hour." **Kayla** gives **Mom** a hug and puts her new **wristwatch** on her arm.

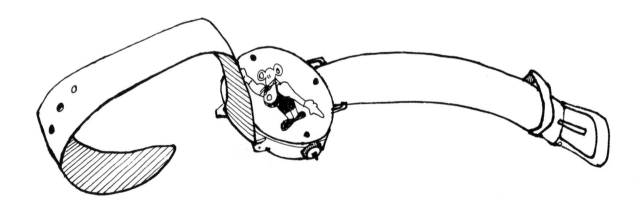

Drama & Music: Creative Activities for Young Children
32

SCAVENGER HUNTS

One of the best ways for children to sharpen their listening skills is through scavenger hunts for sounds. Young listeners often lack the ability to make fine distinctions between sounds. When they are given activities that focus their attention on subtle discriminations, they increase aural acuity considerably. Scavenger hunts require an intense focus but can be extremely enjoyable.

Much like the structure of a traditional scavenger hunt game, the listening task involves "collecting" sounds. The collection process will necessitate a tape recorder and cassette tapes. Most schools have multiple recording units. Further, many children have this technology available in the home.

Sometimes the scavenger hunt will be dispatched as an assignment for homework, following a list of sought sounds. Other times, the activity allows the child to develop the list and tape record freely. Such open architecture to the activity allows an additional creative dimension to the process.

Please allow plenty of discussion time when listening to hunt tapes. The children should be rewarded the "honor" of describing the sounds they captured, much like a fisherman enjoys sharing the details of a catch.

Activities, Activities, Activities

1. LARGE GROUP SOUND HUNTS

Using a cassette tape recorder and blank cassette, record five classroom sounds that are distinctive. For example, if the classroom has a clock, record the ticking sound. If the school bell rings, record the sound. Make a list of the sounds on the chalkboard. Listen to the recording and discuss the characteristics of the sound that "proves" it is that sound.

2. SMALL GROUP SOUND HUNTS

Give teams of children (at least three students) a list of sounds to collect that are similar in genre but different in sound. A set of fire alarm sounds, for example, might include the sound of the fire bell at a school, a fire engine siren, a smoke detector alarm, and so forth. One child should make a list or draw the sound source. Have each team present its tape and discuss the differences between the sounds.
Other genre might include:

> sports/games sounds
> animal sounds
> water sounds
> machine sounds

3. INDIVIDUAL SCAVENGER HUNTS

This assignment works well if children have access to cassette tapes and recorders at home. Ask children to record a set of five sounds from one specific room in their home. They are to make a list but not reveal it to anyone else.

Divide the class into two teams of listeners. Each child then plays his or her tape's sounds one at a time, pausing for the competing team to identify the room in which it was recorded. After one sound is heard, the team gets one chance to identify the source room. If the room is identified after recognizing one sound, the team gets one point. A second sound is played for the next clue if the room has not been identified. Two points are received if the correct answer is given after two sounds and so forth. The game continues until the room is identified. If it is not, the tape is listened to again with sounds being identified by the child who recorded them. After all tapes are analyzed, the team with the lowest score wins.

BODY SOUND ACTIVITIES

Body sound activities can strengthen coordination as well as enhance music skills. We recommend that the body be explored as an "instrument," that is, as a potential source for creative, expressive sound. Children naturally respond to music through body movements which often result in sounds. Help them to refine their gross and fine motor skills while learning about aspects of music.

Keep in mind that some children develop motor skills through different stages of maturity. Further, physically challenged children may have very limited motor skills. We have suggested body sounds that many children may perform, however, you should adapt the specific skills accordingly. The body sounds below may be used throughout the activities in this book. Note the progressive nature of the list:

Kindergarten
• stamping
• patschen (patting thighs)
• clapping
• bopping fists
• rubbing hands

First grade
• snapping fingers
• tipping fingers

Second grade
• clapping (others' hands)

Primary level children are capable of making excellent body sounds using gross motor movements. Especially successful are clapping, stamping, patschen (tapping thighs), tipping (index fingers), bopping (pounding fists on top of one another), and rubbing hands.

Activities, Activities, Activities

1. WARMUP

Concentrate on clapping, patschen and stamping as a group together. Count off four, and have children clap four times, patsch four times, and stamp four times. Try the patterns at various volume levels. As coordination improves, change the speed of the patterns.

2. WHO STOLE THE COOKIE

Learn *Who Stole the Cookie* as a chant. Next, patsch on the accented word or syllable in bold:

Who stole the **cook**ie from the **cook**ie **jar**?

Rodney stole the **cook**ie from the **cook**ie **jar**.

Who **me**?

Yes, **you**.

Couldn't **be**!

Then, **who**?

Every child should have an opportunity to be called upon in the chant and to respond. This is an excellent chant game to challenge the memories of young minds, for they must remember who has been called upon and who remains to be called upon!

Clarify the rhythm of each line of a chant (such as "Who stole the cookie from the cookie jar") by clapping each line individually. Some of the rhythms are uneven and should be performed with that irregularity. Other rhythms are even. Point out the differences to the children. When returning to the patschen (even) beat, listen for the contrast between the uneven rhythms and even beat.

Drama & Music: Creative Activities for Young Children

3. SOUND EFFECTS

Emphasize sound effects of a particular song with body sounds. For example, in *Shoo, Fly* rub hands to make a whooshing sound every time the word "shoo" occurs.

SHOO, FLY

4. BODY SOUND ORCHESTRA

Before children learn to play instruments, they should have many experiences using their bodies to develop the coordination and skill necessary for controlling an instrument. In the following example, a song is changed to a rhythmic chant to concentrate on the expressive use of the body to hear and feel different rhythms.

Bingo traditionally involves the incremental clapping and silent voicing of the rhythm:

for B- I- NG - O. However, the entire song may involve other body sounds. To illustrate different body sounds for the rhythm, see below.

Bop: There was a farmer had a dog and

Stamp: Bingo was his name-o.

Clap: B - I - NG - O, B - I - NG - O, B - I - NG - O (and)

Stamp: Bingo was his name-o.

For additional activities with this song see page 58.

Drama & Music: Creative Activities for Young Children

ADDITIONAL IDEAS

• Sing the familiar song and add body sound orchestra by designating half of the group as singers and the other half as "orchestra" players.

BINGO

TRADITIONAL

Rhythmically

There was a farm - er had a dog and

Bin - go was his name - o. B - I - N - G - O, B - I -

N - G - O, B - I - N - G - O And Bin - go was his name - o.

VOCAL SOUNDS

Developing the voice for speech and language arts usage has obvious merits. We'd like, however, to explore the voice as an expressive instrument – that goes beyond articulating words clearly. In fact, when you consider the whole range of sounds within the realm of vocal noises, words are just a portion of the possibilities! Humming, buzzing, tongue clicking, whistling, lip popping, to name a few, also convey meanings and can be very expressive.

Vocal sounds may be approached any number of ways. You might start with the spoken word, such as words in a poem, and begin to "paint" the words by manipulating the pronunciation to create special effects. For example, additional meaning can be infused into words with different *inflection* (vocal direction), *accent* (stress), *dynamics* (volume), *tempo* (speed), and *articulation* (smooth or detached). Take the word "bombastic," for example. With the proper dynamics, accent, tempo and articulation, you can create a bomb-like effect in merely saying it expressively.

Other ways to achieve "bombastic" effects would be through sound effects using the mouth, tongue, teeth and lips. Ask any second grader to make the sounds of a bomb exploding and he or she will have no difficulty.

Children are especially creative in using vocal sounds. If you channel their efforts, the artistic results in poetry reading, songs, and sound pieces will be most satisfying.

Drama & Music: Creative Activities for Young Children

1. I HEAR YOU

This game gives children five seconds to prepare their sounds, five seconds to make the sound, and five seconds to get ready for the next direction. Begin by "counting" with your fingers while you say,

1. Tongues <u>click</u> and <u>cluck</u> now (five beats for sound).
   Then state: "I hear you".

2. Lips purse to <u>whistle</u> (five beats for sound).
   Then repeat: "I hear you".

3. Cheeks fill with air, <u>blow</u>. (Etc.)

4. <u>Gar-gle</u> all a- round.

5. Bees <u>buzz</u> high and low.

6. Winds <u>blow</u> fierce and fast.

7. Rain <u>plops</u> down loud-ly.

8. <u>Mist</u> falls down slow-ly.

9. Small <u>bub-bles</u> sur-face.

10. Si-rens <u>scream</u> up high.

FOUND SOUNDS

Found sounds are any sounds you can find or make in your environment. Notice, we have avoided using the term "noise" in this definition. For creative purposes, we want to develop a sound palette with sensitivity to sound. By that we mean, found sound has special creative purpose. The sounds are carefully controlled and used for special effects. They are not random, mindless noises made to fill up periods of silence.

Typically, children begin to explore their environment by tapping and shaking items in the classroom. Pencils tap trash cans. Chalk raps windows. Shades rattle. Spiral notebooks get scraped with rulers. Lunch money jingles. These are all good starting places. From the beginning, children need to be centered on discussing the characteristics of the sound produced. Classifying the sounds as high/low; soft/loud; long/short; or bright/dark, will bring along their aural skills. It is also a good idea after discovering sounds to use them immediately in a rhythmic context. For example, ask the children to play the sound in the rhythm of the opening phrase of *Happy Birthday*.

In this book, some of the found sound activities are prescriptive in that they require sounds from a particular environment, such as a kitchen or garage. On other occasions, the found sounds might involve bringing objects to school that make interesting sounds, such as coat hangers, old keys, or plastic aerosol can tops. Given the opportunity to search for and find unusual sounds will stretch the children's awareness of sound characteristics.

Finally, please consider found sounds as an orchestra in themselves – they can be classified into groups of high and low or metal and nonmetal. The instruments can perform rhythm pieces as in a band or accompany songs, stories and poems beautifully.

Drama & Music: Creative Activities for Young Children

1. SOUND BOXES

Bring a box of items to the classroom which have potential to make sounds. Ask the children to "find" sounds by shaking, tapping, or scraping the item (without damaging anything). After initial exploration of different sounds, ask each child to say his or her name and then make the sound in the rhythm of his or her name.

IDEAS FOR FOUND SOUND BOXES:

Sewing Box
- Scissors
- Various sizes of spools of thread
- Tape measures
- Needles in small plastic boxes
- Darning forms
- Elastic strips of various lengths
- Buttons in jars
- Buttons in various containers
- Pattern paper

Kitchen Gadget Box
- Spatulas
- Egg beaters
- Tongs
- Whisks
- Spoons of various sizes
- Can opener
- Skewers

 ADDITIONAL IDEA

- Ask the children to bring an item from home to make a Sound Box. Consider a:
    - Playground Box (with balls, jump ropes, etc.)
    - Closet Box (old shoes, hangers, etc.)
    - Garden Box (seeds, tools, soil in containers, etc.)

Activities, Activities, Activities

RHYTHM INSTRUMENT ACTIVITIES

For the activities in this category as well as extension ideas for orchestrations, songs and other areas, you will need a basic set of rhythm instruments. Instruments may be purchased in a set, or you can acquire a collection of select instruments on an individual basis. We recommend the following basic set for a classroom with approximately 25 students:

Wood instruments
    rhythm sticks (one set per child)
    drum (at least two good quality ones)
    wood blocks (two or three)
    maracas (two sets)
Metal instruments
    triangles (two or three)
    jingle clogs (two or three)
    finger cymbals (two or three sets)
    hand cymbals (one set)
    tambourines (four or five small ones)

An enhanced set which includes these additional instruments will provide more creative potential:

Wood instruments
    claves (two sets)
    guiro (one)
Metal instruments
    cow bell (one)
    jingle bells (four)
    different sized triangles (four)
    small gong (one)
(See Appendix C for a list of companies offering rhythm instruments.)

We recommend that you introduce children to rhythm instruments one at a time. It is important to model the proper handling of all instruments, particularly when they are modeled for the first time. A new instrument per day seems to give children adequate time to become familiar with it visually and aurally. Allow time for children to play the instrument, learn its name, and know it by sight. With respect to classroom management, it is always a good idea to give directions before distributing instruments. Once the children hold the instruments, the temptation to play them is strong – much stronger than listening for further directions.

Through these activities, you will develop the children's ability to recognize the instruments by ear, improve coordination and fine motor skills, acquire different concepts throughout the curriculum, be expressive and have fun in musicianly ways! Rhythm instruments are a wise investment.

1. SURPRISE SOUND BOX

Once children have met four or five different instruments, they can play Surprise Sound Box. Set up an empty cardboard box large enough to house five different rhythm instruments. Place the box on its side so that the opening of the box is turned away from the children. Invite individual children to play one of the instruments to "surprise" the rest of the children on the other side of the box. The class should identify the instrument by its sound only. Once identified, the child should reinforce by showing and playing the instrument before the group.

2. CLASSROOM INSTRUMENT BANDS

Use the rhythm instruments to play the lines of familiar songs, chants, or rhymes. Each instrument should play a different line. For example, use the rhythm from *Hot Cross Buns*.

Line 1   Rhythm sticks:
>   Hot cross buns!

Line 2   Woodblocks:
>   Hot cross buns!

Line 3   Sand blocks:
>   One-a-penny, two-a-penny,

Line 4   Tambourine:
>   Hot cross buns!

Other songs, chants or rhymes to learn include (music/lyrics in Appendix C):

Baa, Baa Black Sheep   *Little Jack Horner*
Love Somebody   *Looby Loo*
Merrily We Roll Along   *Row, Row, Row Your Boat*
Three Blind Mice

3. SONG TO STORY

Children should be familiar with the following songs. Divide the class into four groups. Select one song per group to be used as the basis for a story creation. Each group should decide what would happen if the song were to continue. The students should create, rehearse, and enact a story that shows the next event.

Hush Little Baby – What will you buy next? Where will you get it? What will happen to it?

Michael, Row Your Boat Ashore – What happens when the boat finally docks? What is the land like and what is discovered there?

Twinkle, Twinkle – Take a trip to the twinkling star. What happens to you there?

Yankee Doodle – What happens to Yankee Doodle when he arrives in town?

Activities, Activities, Activities

ORCHESTRATIONS

Orchestrate familiar rhymes with rhythm instruments. Begin with simple sounding of instruments for particular effects. For example, in *Twinkle, Twinkle, Little Star*, use a small set of cymbals or a triangle to sound on the word "twinkle."

Graduate to more involved orchestrations.

Drama & Music: Creative Activities for Young Children

1. HUMPTY DUMPTY

In *Humpty Dumpty*, children can keep the beat as well as provide interesting sound effects. The following arrangement typifies a primary orchestra:

First, after learning the chant, assign a small group of children to softly keep the beat (underlined) with rhythm instruments:

<u>Hum</u>pty, <u>dump</u>ty, <u>sat</u> on a wall,
<u>Hum</u>pty, <u>dump</u>ty, <u>had</u> a great <u>fall</u>.
<u>All</u> the king's <u>hors</u>es and <u>all</u> the king's <u>men</u>,
<u>Could</u>n't put <u>Hum</u>pty to<u>geth</u>er a<u>gain</u>.

Second, add a drum to sound on the "fall" at the end of line two. Assign one child to perform the "Humpty dumpty" rhythm of the words on a wood block.

We suggest that you practice each step separately before trying to put the orchestra together!

Activities, Activities, Activities

47

2. THE SQUIRREL

Some poems seem to lend themselves to orchestration very easily. Consider the following poem, *The Squirrel*, for its sound potential:

Whisky, frisky
Hippity hop,
Up he goes
To the treetop!

Whirly, twirly,
Round and round,
Down he scampers
To the ground.

Furly, curly
What a tail!
Tall as a feather,
Broad as a sail!
Where's his supper?
In the shell,
Snappity, crackity,
Out it fell!

For the first stanza, encourage children to use high-pitched instruments to orchestrate the direction of the squirrel going to the treetop. Consider the opposite effect for the second stanza.

Select instruments that are easy to manipulate for crisp sounds that might accompany "snappity, crackity" in the shell.

 ADDITIONAL IDEA

• Divide the children into two groups. Have the children in one group orchestrate the poem while the children in the other group pantomime the actions of the squirrel.

3. WISHES

Some instrumental experiences should allow children to play instruments freely and explore a whole new palette of sound. *Wishes* has potential for creative exploration but is quite lengthy; therefore, a good suggestion is to split up the poem by stanzas.

Said the first little chicken
with a queer little squirm,
"I wish I could find
a fat little worm."

Said the second little chicken
With an odd little shrug,
"I wish I could find
a fat little slug."

Said the third little chicken
With a sharp little squeal,
"I wish I could find
some nice yellow meal!"

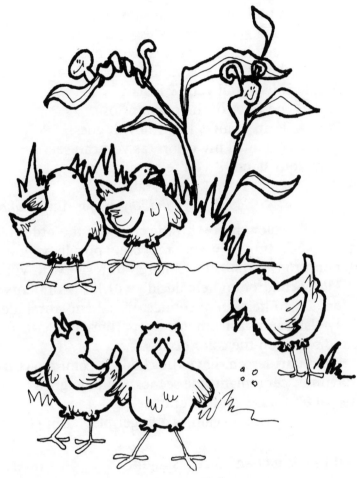

Said the fourth little chicken
With a small sigh of grief,
"I wish I could find
a little green leaf."

Said the fifth little chicken
With a faint little moan,
"I wish I could find
a small gravel stone."

"Now see here," said their mother
From the green garden patch.
"If you want any breakfast,
Just come here and
        SCRATCH!"

Distribute an assortment of classroom instruments and ask children to make sounds to accompany "queer little squirm," "an odd little shrug," "sharp little squeal," "small sigh of grief," and "faint little moan."
Have all instruments perform the final line, "SCRATCH!"

4. COLORS

Read the children the poem, *Colors,* and ask them why the poet may have given the work its title. Other questions could include "What is your favorite color?" " What other things are the color of white, black, brown, etc.?"

> White is day and black is night.
> Brown is pudding that tastes just right.
> Green is the grass that tickles your toes.
> Red is the color of the big clown's nose.
> Blue is the sky on a summer's day.
> Purple is jelly and yellow is hay.
> Pink is the color of the rabbit's nose.
> Orange is an orange, that's how it goes!
> Now I've named my colors, as you can see.
> Clap your hands if you're proud of me!
>> Terry Lynne Graham
>> *Fingerplays and Rhymes for Always and Sometimes*

Make a color chart with the colors in the order of their appearance in the poem: white, black, brown, green, red, blue, purple, yellow, pink, orange. As the poem is recited, point to the colors for children to recite with you.

Allow children to help decide which instruments would be best for the "white" sound. Try to help them connect visual and aural ideas of light and dark sounds. Use as many classroom instruments as appropriate. Perform the poem with the instrument sounding when the color occurs.

For an art lesson, have the children color a picture based on the items in the poem: a daytime scene/nighttime scene, pudding, grass, clown's nose, sky, jar of jelly, bale of hay, rabbit's nose, and an orange.

Now, play *Colors* again as a finger play, using the suggested actions or creating others.

White is day and black is night.	(Start with hands raised and fingers forming a ball for the sun; lower hands on "night")
Brown is pudding that tastes just right.	(Pretend to put spoon to mouth and eat)
Green is the grass that tickles your toes.	(Point to toes)
Red is the color of the big clown's nose.	(Point to nose and laugh)
Blue is the sky on a summer's day.	(Point up)
Purple is jelly and yellow is hay.	(Pantomime spreading jelly on bread) (Put a piece of straw behind ear)
Pink is the color of the rabbit's nose.	(Twitch nose)
Orange is an orange, that's how it goes!	(Pantomime peeling and eating orange)
Now I've named my colors, as you can see.	
Clap your hands if you're proud of me!	(Clap)

SOUND JOURNALS

The listening abilities of children can be furthered through the maintenance of a sound journal. The journal can be as simple as ten pages of 8 1/2 X 11 inch paper folded in half and stapled. Children enter the date of the sound experience and begin writing about or drawing what they heard. They are taken with the experience of keeping a journal – a personal place to write and think about sound. Although many children may not aspire to become performing musicians or composers, they often have the desire to understand and write music – or at least write down some music they have heard or improvised.

With second and third graders, we have used the simple format as illustrated below:

Today's date:

What did you hear?

What did it sound like?

What did the sound look like? (Draw it.)

We ask that the children write in complete sentences, although they do not need to write many sentences.

The sound journal gives children some freedom in recording and expressing what they hear. The process avoids standard notation. Rather, it encourages graphic representation. Please note, pictorial representation is not desirable here. When children hear a soft melody, we do not encourage drawing fluffy kittens. Rather, we encourage them to show the melodic direction using a soft, wavy line in a pastel color.

A sound journal is a place to record what children have heard *using their words*. They are asked to describe the sound from their frame of reference. They also should draw what the sound looks like as they have experienced it. This activity is a perceptual one which can not be judged as "right" or "wrong," although we highly recommend that you read the journals. Most children take the sound journal experience seriously. If some children seem to have difficulty, we ask a child who is confident about his or her entry to share it for the entire class. This modeling seems to help children get on track quickly.

A good place to introduce the sound journal is after scavenger hunt listening. Sounds can be tape-recorded and re-listened to for extra practice. We recommend that you guide the children with a few example entries in the journal as a class. The children should always frame their own sentences and draw their own pictures. Your role is one of asking the children questions to guide their entries, such as: "How would *you* describe this sound? What kind of a character is it? Does it have a shape? Where is it going? Is it heavy or light?"'

Every day should include an entry in the sound journal. Sometimes it is appropriate to take the journal along on a field trip, such as a visit to the fire station, to record unusual sounds. Later, the children can describe and draw them.

Consider the following activities for sound journal work:

1. the voices of your family members
2. the sounds of your pets
3. found sounds discovered in various rooms
4. scavenger hunt sounds collected on cassette tape
5. the sounds of instruments
6. the sounds of machines
7. sounds heard at the zoo
8. sounds made by toys
9. sounds heard on videotapes or television
10. choral music sounds

Drama & Music: Creative Activities for Young Children

1. HIGH TECH SOUNDS

Have the children listen to the processing sounds of a FAX machine, its processing sounds of the printed page, and the distinct click as it shuts down. They might enter those sounds in their journals as such:

Today I heard a FAX machine.
The sound started with five high beeps.
It looks like this:

The next sound was the printing machine.
The sound was kind of a hum and gargle.
It looks like this:

The machine then shut down.
The sound was a clickety-click.
It looks like this:

2. SOUNDS "PAINTED" BY POETRY

Another entry into sound journals can be in the form of poetry, i.e., a poetic picture of the sound. Consider *Animal Rhymes* by Terry Lynne Graham.

Cats purr,
to be sure.

Mice squeak,
to speak.

Horses neigh,
to say.

Hens cluck,
for luck.

Wolves howl,
and prowl.

Kids walk,
and talk!

> Terry Lynne Graham
> *Fingerplays and Rhymes for Always and Sometimes*

 ADDITIONAL IDEAS

• Invite children to compose brief entries describing sounds they hear. Whether they live in a quiet rural setting or a bustling urban city, their environments are full of sounds that can be described through graphic notation or poetic lines.
• Divide the children into three groups. Have one group recite the poem *Animal Rhymes*, while another group pantomimes the animals. The third group should hold up their journal entries for each stanza as it is spoken.

Activities, Activities, Activities

SONGS

We have selected songs that are "winners" in two respects. First, they are songs which have the proper vocal range. This means most young voices will easily be able to sing the melodies in tune. Be sure to give the children a starting pitch or the opening phrase of the song so that they hear and feel the tonal center of it. You may wish to use a pitch pipe, however, sing or hum the tone as well.

The second reason these songs are winners is because they contain interesting rhythms, melodies and lyrics. Many early childhood songs have a good deal of repetition. The more the song repeats, the more the children seem to enjoy it! The songs might be silly scenarios, contain nonsense words, or tell folk tales in comical ways. These songs truly restore the joy of early childhood through music.

Please remember to start the songs with some rhythmic preparation. A number of the songs have a duple or quadruple meter signature at the start: 2/4 or 4/4 respectively on the first line of music. When the songs begin on the first beat, simply sing: "1 - 2 - read-y - go" on the opening pitch. The speed at which you sing those beats will establish the tempo of the song. If it is a fast song, sing the preparatory beats quickly.

Songs in triple meter (3/4 signature) will need three beats of preparation. Sing, "1 - read-y - sing. "

Songs that have motions may be approached in different ways. Usually, it is best to learn the song without any distractions. Some songs, however, have motions that help teach the lyrics. Often it is wise to sing through the song at least once for the children without motions. The second modeling can include the motions. Always sing through the song a couple of times before inviting the children to join you.

To help the children listen carefully while you sing the song, give them two questions so they are attentive to the song's action. The questions might address specific aspects of the lyrics (for example, "How many times did I sing 'shoo fly' in this song? Listen again and count.") Or, the questions may address the musical aspects (for example, "Do you feel a marching beat in this song? Listen and see if a marching beat would fit.")

Please review songs often! And don't forget to take a list of the songs the children know when you are on the bus for a field trip.

1. WHERE IS THUMBKIN? *(to the tune of Are You Sleeping?)*

Where is thumbkin? Where is thumbkin?
Here I am! Here I am!
How are you today, sir? Very well, I thank you.
Run away. Run away.

Motions:

Line 1: Both hands behind back.
Line 2: Bring one hand to front, presenting thumb. Follow same with second hand.
Line 3: Wiggle one thumb. "Answer" with the other thumb.
Line 4: Move one hand behind back. Follow with the second.

Repeat motions for verse two (index finger), three (middle man), four (ring finger), and five (pinky). For verse six, use the whole hand.

 ADDITIONAL IDEA

• Because this song has some repetition in it, it is a good song for children to listen carefully to the teacher's voice for an appropriate vocal model. Perform the song as an echo song, with the teacher alternating the phrases with the children.

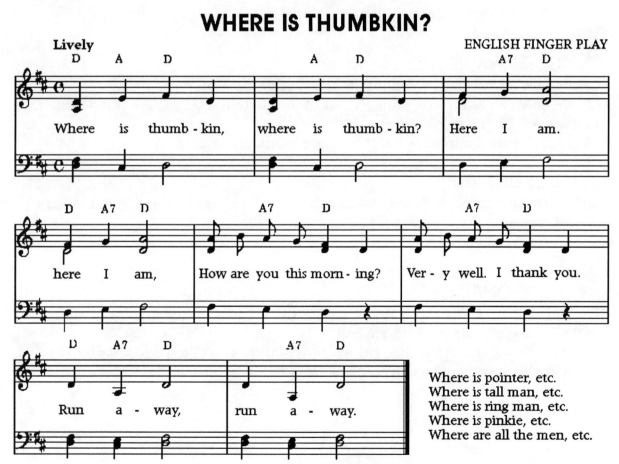

Where is pointer, etc.
Where is tall man, etc.
Where is ring man, etc.
Where is pinkie, etc.
Where are all the men, etc.

Activities, Activities, Activities

2. SHOO, FLY

This song has three parts. Notice that the "shoo, fly" section returns after the contrasting middle part. To help children hear and feel the differences between the parts, bring to their attention the way it is organized.

ADDITIONAL IDEAS

• Add motions to the "shoo" section.
• Discuss what a morning star is.
• Add instruments to orchestrate the "shoo" sound. For example, rub sand blocks or scrape rhythm sticks for a special effect.
• An additional activity involving this song is found on page 37.

3. BINGO

This is a good song to help children hear and feel differences between beat and rhythm. When children clap to B - I - NG - O, they are clapping a rhythm pattern:

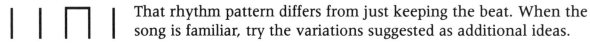 That rhythm pattern differs from just keeping the beat. When the song is familiar, try the variations suggested as additional ideas.

ADDITIONAL IDEAS

• Create new names for the dog that fit the rhythm pattern.
• Create new names for new animals that fit the rhythm, e.g., "There was a farmer, had a cat and PUFFY was her name-o."
• Additional activities involving this song are found on page 38.

4. YANKEE DOODLE

The first time through *Yankee Doodle*, ask the children some listening questions so they will pay attention to the words. For example, "What did Yankee Doodle stick in his cap? What did he call it?"

ADDITIONAL IDEAS

• Feel the beat by marching to *Yankee Doodle*. Get the feet started first by chanting "1 - 2 - 1 - 2 - left - right - here-we go!"
• Try marching and keeping the beat with rhythm sticks while singing *Yankee Doodle*.
• Share the history contained in this American folk tune.

YANKEE DOODLE

With martial precision

English-American Folk Song

OTHER SUREFIRE SONGS

The list below contains songs that are in the correct vocal range, easily accessible, and fun for young children. Many of the previous extension ideas can be applied to them as well. See Appendix C for music and lyrics.

Blue Bird
Farmer in the Dell
Ring Around the Rosy
Rain, Rain Go Away
Twinkle, Twinkle Little Star

Bye, Baby Bunting
Hot Cross Buns
Sally Go 'Round the Moon
This Old Man

Activities, Activities, Activities

CONCENTRATION GAMES

Being attentive and staying on task are critical to success in drama and in school. Concentration games provide practice in focusing upon what is happening and mentally marking the details. The more children play these games, the more adept they should become at retaining information and blocking out distractions.

To play concentration games, children commonly sit or stand in a circle. In one popular format, children add to a list of items. One person begins by naming one thing, the next repeats it and adds his or her own, the next person repeats and adds, and so on until all have had a chance. You may either go from one child to the next around the circle, or call on children in a random pattern. As they become more skilled, children may wish to call upon each other.

Some teaching tips are offered here. Please remember that creative drama is process rather than product oriented and that means that the benefit that the child derives from an activity is paramount. There should be no winners and losers in creative drama games. Even when elimination from the game is a part of an activity's structure, no child should be made to feel that he or she has failed. For this reason, when doing concentration games, should a child forget something in the sequence, draw a blank when it comes to adding information, or make a mistake, we recommend encouraging others to help by giving hints, pantomiming objects, or repeating information. Do, however, give the child a chance to respond and be alert to those in your class who might want to "help" before assistance is actually needed. A child who is truly at a loss, however, should not be made to feel uncomfortable. If this happens, simply skip to the next person. You may either pick up where you left off or start a new sequence.

When doing concentration games with very young children, consider playing in small groups. It is easier for young ones, for example, to remember six objects than twenty-six. As children become older and their attention spans and retention abilities expand, concentration games can become more complex and challenging. Help the children to recognize that the desired outcome of a concentration game is to remember successfully, not to stump one another. Commend children when they are able to complete an entire series or sequence and, if they can go around the circle more than once, so much the better!

Notable among the many skills cultivated when children play concentration games are listening, memory development and teamwork. You may also recognize the structure of the concentration game in other activities, such as some name games and some story creation exercises.

1. MOM SENT ME TO THE STORE TO BUY...

Use this activity to combine a concentration game and math facts. The children are seated in a circle. The teacher begins by saying, "Mom sent me to the store to buy," and names an object and an appropriate measurement for that item. The person to the teacher's left repeats the phrase, the teacher's object, and then adds an object. This continues with each child repeating the phrase, previously named objects, and then adding an item. Should a child have difficulty remembering the list, allow other students to provide gentle reminders. Consider the following example:

Teacher: Mom sent me to the store to buy three inches of ribbon.

Child: Mom sent me to the store to buy three inches of ribbon and a quart of milk.

Child: Mom sent me to the store to buy three inches of ribbon, a quart of milk, and a two liter bottle of soft drink.

Activities, Activities, Activities

MUSICAL PUZZLES, QUESTIONS AND ANSWERS

The activities in this category range from simple echo work to sophisticated critical thinking tasks. You may wish to begin or end creative music sessions with a puzzle. The activities are typically open-ended and can last for two or twenty-two minutes, depending upon the attention span of the children.

Once you are familiar with the basic activity, you can apply it to different contexts (using body sounds, found sounds, vocal sounds or instrumental sounds) and various grade levels.

1. ECHO

Clap the following rhythmic patterns for children to imitate. *Teaching suggestion: gesture to the children at the close of the pattern a signal for them to begin the echo.*

Teacher   Children

ADDITIONAL IDEAS
- Vary the body sound. Stamp some patterns, patschen others.
- Invite children to create patterns for the class to echo.
- Try echo patterns using different instruments or found sounds in the classroom.

Activities, Activities, Activities

61

2. RHYTHMIC QUESTIONS AND ANSWERS

Children can get the feel of a rhythmic "conversation" by playing rhythmic instruments in question and answer formats. For example, place the rhythms below on the chalkboard. Practice all patterns as a group. Distribute rhythm instruments to pairs of children and have them practice the following sample patterns to experience a suggested length and tempo for questions and answers. Then allow the pairs to reverse roles, with the responder taking the lead.

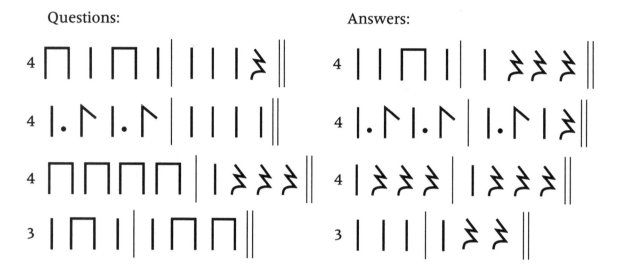

3. MUSICAL MYSTERIES

Invite children to play the rhythm of a familiar song for the class to identify. Practice with some patterns which the children will immediately recognize, such as *Happy Birthday*, *Are You Sleeping*, or *Jingle Bells*.

MOVEMENT

Fundamental movements are identified as walking, skipping, jumping and hopping and basic locomotor movements which at first glance do not seem to be creative. Practice with fundamental movements, however, is necessary for creative movement to succeed. First, children need to develop a repertory of movements from which to draw when they respond to rudimentary drama and music activities creatively. Second, children can learn to be expressive through familiar movements. The goal for the teacher of young children is to strike a balance between spontaneous, free movements and teacher-directed activities.

We offer the following guidelines to help you be successful in facilitating movement sessions:

(a) Since children are highly imitative – both in improvised and directed movement activities – occasionally ask them to close their eyes to think up new movements and perform them.

(b) Provide plenty of practice for revisiting fundamental movements. These may appear simple, but they are the building blocks to movement development. Package the review sessions in fresh ways. For example, instead of just asking the children to crawl, announce that today we are going to crawl like dinosaurs who have been in a cave for six million years.

(c) Encourage students to maintain their balance and strive for staying with the beat or tempo (speed) of the activity. Ask them to think about and to demonstrate different ways to execute the same movement. Though the movements involved are not new, the child should experience them anew – for expressive purposes.

(d) To keep the movements together and the children on task when coordinating movement and music, use a small hand drum to establish a beat. A moderate tempo works best. Tell children the beat means "on." When the beat stops, they are "off" and must freeze to listen. Similarly, in drama, allow time for the movement and again rely upon "freeze" or a similar cue to pause the action.

(e) With tape or chalk, outline various shapes or configurations on the floor or playground. Ask children to move on the lines like a wave, a sharp angle, or straight line, depending on the shape of the figures. If space is limited, provide a shape-space for each child in or on which to create. This solves some of the safety concerns.

(f) Always allow adequate space for movement activities and remind children to be sensitive to and aware of their own and their neighbors' personal spaces.

(g) Join in as a co-explorer! Though the children are apt to imitate your movements at the beginning, you can establish a positive and creative example in your own explorations.

Activities, Activities, Activities

1. WARMUP

From the list of fundamental movements below, select four to rehearse in one session:

walk	jump	slide	skip	march
turn	stretch	twist	swing	bend
balance	push	pull	hop	glide
trot	gallop	crawl		

Count to four and beat the drum for sixteen beats, with the direction to WALK for sixteen beats. Directions then continue: Stop, change direction and get ready for the second movement: JUMP. After four preparation counts, JUMP for sixteen beats. Continue with additional movements.

Adjust the tempo (speed) by going through the same patterns to experience speed walking and slow-motion walking. Point out to the children the various ways people hold their heads, swing their arms, move their hips, raise their feet, and bend their backs while walking. Have them explore these variations while keeping the walking pattern simple.

Each subsequent movement session may introduce two or three additional fundamental movements to practice. Soon, you will be able to warmup with eight different movements, during 128 beats (sixteen beats for each movement)!

2. BEAN BAG BONG

Each child needs a bean bag for these movements. The goal is to help children coordinate hand skills while other activities (physical and mental) occur. Denim bags (approximately three inches square) filled with raw beans work well. To help keep movements together, use a small hand drum to establish a moderate speed. Sixteen beat units for each movement give adequate practice time. Count to four for "get ready" beats!

Ask the children to keep the beat by tossing the bean bag from hand to hand:
1. while standing,
2. while sitting,
3. while kneeling;
4. while chanting *Hickory Dickory Dock*. Notice that the bag gets tossed during the chanting of words and during silence. Keep the beat steady.
5. while chanting *Five Little Monkeys*.
6. while marching to *Yankee Doodle*.

Drama & Music: Creative Activities for Young Children

3. FIND MY PARTNER ANIMAL CARDS

Prior to playing, the teacher should prepare two identical sets of cards. On each card, there is a picture of an animal. Each set, for example, may be comprised of pictures of a horse, elephant, cow, dog, pig, owl, frog, bear, lion, and monkey. Divide the class into two groups and invite players to select a card, each group selecting from one of the sets. The groups should then line up, one on each side of the room. At the teacher's signal, the children travel across the room, moving like and making the sound of their animal. They look for the person in the other group who is moving in the same way and making the same sound. Play ends when all of the children find their partners.

Drama & Music: Creative Activities for Young Children

Activities, Activities, Activities

67

4. LITTLE DUCK

To play *Little Duck*, ask the children to stand in a circle and participate with sound and motion.

Little duck, little duck
Waddling all the day.
Little duck, little duck
Waddling while you play.

Little duck, little duck
Quacking all the day.
Little duck, little duck
Quacking while you play.

Little duck, little duck
Swimming all the day.
Little duck, little duck
Swimming while you play.

5. CREATIVE INTERPRETATION

The next poems begin to move children from literal to free movements. They suggest types of movements and they may be done to the metrical flow of the poem, or they can be entirely free expressions. Lengthier poems present more room for expressive movement. The following poem involves responding to the movements of a partner. Ask the children to close their eyes while listening.

Snakes slither,
I shiver.

As they slide,
I hide.

I know that I
Should really try

Not to shake
Around a snake.

Terry Lynne Graham
Fingerplays and Rhymes for Always and Sometimes

Read the poem for the children and ask them to visualize how they would move if they were the child. Repeat the poem and ask them to visualize how they would move if they were the snake.

Assign children to be the child or the snake. Watch for key words that suggest special movements and help the children plan their movements with "slither," "shiver," "slide," "hide," and "shake".

Ask children to find a partner and perform *Snakes*. Change roles and move again.

All children will be able to relate emotionally to this poem. It will be fun to show emotions through movement!

Children will enjoy acting out the puffing, snuffing, roaring, and snoring in the next poem, *Jeremiah Obadiah*. The poem has many sounds children will have fun making. We suggest that the teacher ask the children to listen carefully to the poem as it is read. Next, have the children move as the teacher narrates the poem. Replay the poem, encouraging the children to add sounds in addition to movement.

Jeremiah Obadiah, puff, puff, puff,
When he gives his messages he snuffs, snuffs, snuffs,
When he goes to school by day, he roars, roars, roars,
When he goes to bed at night he snores, snores, snores,
When he goes to Christmas treat he eats plum-duff,
Jeremiah Obadiah, puff, puff, puff.

Activities, Activities, Activities

BODY SCULPTURES AND LIVING PICTURES

Many fundamental and creative movements can be incorporated into body sculptures and living pictures, although once selected the movements or positions are held in a freeze. These two types of activities are based upon art forms, the earlier being statues and the latter being paintings or photographs.

In both, one player begins by taking a position and holding it. When other children see how they might add to the overall work, they join and freeze in position. No single child is responsible for an entire element. The activities help to illustrate how parts combine to make a whole. The primary difference between these activities is that *body sculptures* tend to work best for showing abstract concepts like emotions, while *living pictures* are more effective with concrete images like a beach scene. In both, there should be no limitation placed upon the number of children who can be a part of the artistic product. You may, however, wish to add stipulations like touch or don't touch body parts, take only vertical positions, etc.

We recommend using these activities to develop physical skills, teach abstract and concrete concepts, and introduce or reinforce artistic applications such as identifying foreground, background, and eye path.

Drama & Music: Creative Activities for Young Children

1. SHAPES

For this activity, you will need to make a set of four shapes for each child.

Rectangle	Circle
Square	Triangle

Let the children connect the shapes by pasting them in any arrangement they choose. Place their names on the final shaped work. Select one child's work and ask the other children to observe it carefully. Then, ask the children to use their bodies to re-create what they see. The number of children engaged in making the body sculpture will depend upon the construction being modeled. This activity can be repeated often, using other classmates' works as the basis of the body sculptures.

2. THE STORE

Have the children create living pictures of stores. They might, for example, create one of a grocery store or a clothing store. Included in the living picture should be people who might work and shop there as well as objects which would identify the place.

3. NOW YOU SEE IT, NOW YOU DON'T

Emphasis here is on accurate replication of ball size, shape, weight, etc., as well as the rotational pattern. You'll need a collection of balls, such as a softball, kickball, football, and beachball. With the children standing in a circle, select one of the balls. Move it around the circle in a random pattern by passing, tossing, rolling, or bouncing it. Then, remove the ball and repeat the pattern, maintaining the size, shape, weight, etc. with an imaginary ball. Repeat this as many times as you like, using a different ball each time.

Next, invite the children to make body sculptures of the following emotional responses.

- Excitement at scoring the winning run at the softball game.
- Anger at missing a catch at the kickball game.
- Joy at kicking the winning field goal at the football game.
- Worry at watching your beachball float away.

 ADDITIONAL IDEA

- Make living pictures of the following places.
  a football game
  a playground
  a beach
  a ball field

CREATIVE MOVEMENT

Flexibility, clarity and mastery in physical endeavors are desirable in creative drama and should be nurtured from the earliest sessions. It is often advantageous to work on activities which promote development of physical aptitude and agility before concentrating upon voice work. When children are not self-conscious about how they look, they are more free to respond creatively and to then incorporate dialogue naturally. Creative movement activities take advantage of the child's natural ability to utilize gross motor skills and should be considered as preparatory for pantomime and later, more complex character work.

Drama & Music: Creative Activities for Young Children

1. MACHINES I

Children can have fun re-creating machines with which they are familiar or inventing new ones by using their bodies as components. One child comes to the center of the room and begins a motion, such as bending up and down. Another child joins with a new motion. Each child continues to make his or her motion while other children join. This process continues until several children are involved, each contributing a new motion. The "machine" should then freeze and those who have created it should be asked to identify the kind of machine it is. What does it do or make?

 ADDITIONAL IDEA

• Add a sound as well as a motion.

2. MACHINES II

Consult Machines I for basic instructions. With more advanced children, concentrate on making machines of the future. What fascinating devices are likely to be in use? At this level, the teacher should actively encourage as many children to join as have ideas as to how they might fit into the invention. Play with motion only or with sound and motion.

3. TEXTURE WALK

During this exercise, the children are to walk in a circle and to imagine that the surface is changing beneath them. The teacher calls out a surface and the children physically demonstrate walking on or through it. Stimulate imaginations through the use of sidecoaching comments (rhetorical questions or statements designed to deepen involvement). The activity is most effective when players use imagination, sensory awareness, and physicalization. We suggest using the following direction to conduct the exercise.

Teacher: Begin by walking normally on the ground. Now, the surface is changing. The ground is covered with:

jello	peanut butter
snow	deep water
mud	sand
hot coals	pudding
glue	ice

The surface can also be changed by making it a weightless environment, very hot, very cold, windy, etc. You and your children will enjoy adding to this list and thinking about how the body moves through space.

4. TWIN ROBOTS

The children should work in pairs and should face each other. Moving as robots, one child should engage in a series of movements, such as moving an arm, a leg, the other arm, and so forth and the other child should try to move with the partner. The goal of this activity is to have the children synchronize their movements so closely that an observer can't tell which child has started the movement. It's important to play this in pantomime, as talking minimizes the levels of trust and concentration that the exercise is designed to strengthen. While the children are learning the exercise and building concentration skills (Don't be surprised if they giggle a lot at first!), determine who will start before beginning to play. As the children's skills improve, they will be able to alternate the introduction of new movements.

Drama & Music: Creative Activities for Young Children

PANTOMIME

In creative drama, pantomime is the expression of feelings, actions and ideas through physical means. The body, not the voice, is the instrument of communication.

Several teaching tips will facilitate the teacher's work in pantomime. Most important is the need for action. There must be something for the children to do or respond to emotionally and for this reason you will see pantomime activities framed with "Show me" or a similar active directive. Inactive verbs encourage a lack of creative participation. Second, be certain that the children understand that clarity, not fooling their classmates or inappropriately keeping the attention of their peers, is the desired goal. A successful pantomime is one that children recognize. Third, do not confuse these activities with the more precise art of mime. Because creative drama is process oriented rather than product centered, the children should not be assessed by standards for skills beyond their level of development. Fourth, we encourage the introduction of pantomime prior to concentrating upon verbal activities because we believe that when a child is comfortable with his or her physical capabilities, that youngster will be less self-conscious and better able to focus upon more complex activities that merge physical and verbal interpretations.

Should the activity be stopped if the children speak or make sounds during a pantomime? You will have to make a decision if the children are verbal. Sounds related to the activity, such as pantomiming a kitten and purring, are often indicative of the child's involvement and should be accepted. If, however, children are giggling or chatting and their talk is unrelated to the pantomime, a reminder about the use of the body and not the voice to communicate may be in order.

The term "narrative pantomime" is found in this text. This simply means that the teacher or some other person narrates while the children pantomime the action. With some classes, you may wish to narrate once or twice before playing occurs so that children are familiar with the content and know what to expect. With other classes, this will seem unnecessary and you will want to move immediately to combining narration and action. In either case, the narrator should be familiar enough with the material to be able to keep an eye on the children, as watching will dictate how much time to allow for their ideas before next speaking. Sidecoaching and replay are helpful techniques to incorporate.

We suggest moving from simple beginning activities to more demanding work. Typically, pantomimes progress from simple introductory activities to pantomime sentences to pantomime paragraphs to narrative pantomime stories. Regardless of the length of the activity, be certain that there is something for the child to physically express. Just as in a language arts analysis, help the children to understand that words lead to sentences, sentences to paragraphs, and paragraphs to stories. In pantomime, the number of physically expressive opportunities should grow as the material expands.

Activities, Activities, Activities

1. YOU ARE A DUCK

Young children enjoy imitating animals. The following pantomime sentences ask them to imagine that they are ducks. All of the pantomimes include "Show me" to insure action.

You are a baby duckling hatching from an egg. Show me how you hatch.

Now, show me how you fly. Next, flap your wings and land.

Show me what you look like when you are searching for food.

You have found something good to eat at the bottom of the pond. Show me what you look like when you dive for the food and then bring it to the surface.

Show me what you look like when you are swimming.

Show me what you look like when you waddle on the banks of the pond.

2. I CAN DO IT

Actions can be written on cards or picture cards can be used. The child picks a card and then pantomimes that action. The other children guess what the player is doing.

I can tie my shoes.
I can dress myself.
I can set the table.
I can help my mom.
I can ride a tricycle.
I can wash my face and comb my hair.
I can brush my teeth.
I can pick up my toys.
I can pack my lunch box.
I can pour my milk into a glass.
I can count from one to ten.
I can print my name.

Drama & Music: Creative Activities for Young Children

3. MY GRANDMA IS SPECIAL

We suggest playing this narrative pantomime in pairs. The activity can also be replayed so that children may switch roles.

My Grandma is special.

Sometimes Grandma stays home with me when my Momma goes to work.

Sometimes Grandma and I bake chocolate chip cookies. Grandma always pours milk for me to drink when I eat my cookies.

Sometimes Grandma and I go for a walk. We like to look in the store windows. We like to stop for sodas before we go home.

Sometimes Grandma reads to me. I like to sit close to her and look at the pictures in the book. I like the sound of Grandma's voice.

Sometimes Grandma lets me help her set the table. When she tells me that I am a good helper, I feel so proud!

Sometimes Grandma buys me presents. She likes to surprise me.

Always, Grandma tucks me into bed. She hugs me and then turns off the bedroom light and turns on the night light.

My Grandma is special.

 ADDITIONAL IDEAS

• After completing play, ask the children to add to this list by identifying a favorite relative and the things that he or she does that are special. Replay using the newly created list of special actions.
• Ask the children how they refer to their grandparents. Children from a Greek background, for example, may call their Grandma, "Ya Ya." This presents a good opportunity to broaden children's ethnic understanding.

4. CHARACTER WALK

The goals of this exercise are to quickly imagine and convert a mental image into physical form and to introduce physical characterization.

Call out the name of a character and tell the children to physically show the first image of that person that comes to mind. When most or all of the children have responded, another character should be called. Suggested roles might include an astronaut, a cowboy or cowgirl, a cook, a cab driver, a construction worker, a ballerina, a beauty contest entrant, and a soldier. New characters should be added to the list and the children challenged by increasingly fast calls for change.

5. WHAT TIME IS IT?

This activity is played in groups of three. Two children position themselves as the hands of a clock. We suggest stipulating that the time be on the hour or on the half hour. The third child pantomimes an action that is appropriate to the time. The pair forming the hands of the clock, for example, might position themselves to show six o'clock and the child pantomiming might demonstrate eating dinner. The other children in the class guess the time and the action.

Drama & Music: Creative Activities for Young Children

6. PLAYLAND PIZZA PARLOR

This can be played in one of two ways. One method is to have a child sit facing the other children. After the emotional statement has been narrated, the child nonverbally shows the feeling inherent in the statement. After the refrain, the other children imitate that expression. In the second method of playing, all of the children create a facial expression appropriate to their individual responses to the verse. In either approach, the teacher or students can narrate or the teacher or an individual student can speak the first two lines and the class can, in unison, speak the refrain.

I'm going to a birthday party at Playland Pizza Parlor. I'm really excited.
I show that feeling on my face.

My parents are driving me to the birthday party. They're taking a long time to get ready. I'm impatient.
I show that feeling on my face.

We take a long ride to Playland Pizza Parlor. I'm bored.
I show that feeling on my face.

We arrive at the restaurant. My parents drop me off and I go inside. I don't see my friends. I'm nervous.
I show that feeling on my face.

I find my friends. I give my birthday friend a present. I hope my friend likes it.
I show that feeling on my face.

My friend likes my present. I'm glad.
I show that feeling on my face.

I see a room filled with balls. I go there and bounce up and down on the balls. I bounce very high. I feel scared.
I show that feeling on my face.

Next, I play a game at the arcade and win a big prize. I feel proud.
I show that feeling on my face.

It's time to eat. I eat a lot of pizza, ice cream and cake. I enjoy these foods.
I show that feeling on my face.

My stomach hurts. I ate too fast. I don't feel good.
I show that feeling on my face.

It's time to sing *Happy Birthday*. I feel silly.
I show that feeling on my face.

Next, I watch a show. It's funny and I laugh. I am amused.
I show that feeling on my face.

Now it's time to go home. My parents pick me up and I climb into our car. I feel tired.
I show that feeling on my face.

I'm sad that the party is over.
I show that feeling on my face.

I had fun at Playland Pizza Parlor. I hope my parents will let me have my birthday party there.
I show that feeling on my face.

7. COMMUNITY HELPERS

Prepare a set of cards consisting of such community helpers as police officer, fire fighter, and librarian. Depending upon the reading level of the children, cards may have a picture and the name of the helper or simply the picture. Each child draws a card. He or she is given thinking time and then uses an autobiographical approach to describe the character, ending the description with, "Who am I?" The child should not directly state the character's function. Guide children away from descriptions such as, "I am the mail carrier." Instead, encourage depictions such as, "I bring letters and bills and magazines to people's homes and businesses everyday. Who am I?" The other children then identify the community helper.

Drama & Music: Creative Activities for Young Children

Activities, Activities, Activities
81

8. NARRATIVE PANTOMIME POEM

Ask the children to pantomime the actions of Old King Cole, the fifers, the drummer boy, the trumpeters, and the conductor.

Old King Cole was a merry old soul,
And a merry old soul was he;
He called for his pipe,
And he called for his bowl,
And he called for his fiddlers three.

Then he called for his fifers two,
And they puffed and they blew tootle-oo;
And King Cole laughed as his glass he quaffed,
And his fifers puffed tootle-oo.

Then he called for his drummer boy,
The army's pride and joy,
And the thuds out-rang with a loud bang! bang!
The noise of the noisiest toy.

Then he called for his trumpeters four,
Who stood at his own palace door,
And they played trang-a-tang
Whilst the drummer went bang,
And King Cole he called for more.

He called for a man to conduct,
Who into his bed had been tuck'd,
And he had to get up without bite or sup
And waggle his stick and conduct.

Old King Cole laughed with glee,
Such rare antics to see;
There never was man in merry England
Who was half as merry as he.

 ADDITIONAL IDEAS

• Creative movement and art can be incorporated into this activity by having the children make homemade instruments. A drum, for instance, can be concocted from a cylinder oats cereal box. Two paper plates filled with beans and glued together serve as a shaker. Instruments need not be fancy to be fun. Children will enjoy becoming an orchestra and playing their musical creations.

• Switch from an orchestra to a band and stage a parade in the classroom. If the parade activity is one that the children wish to frequently revisit, consider having them "play" familiar songs or original compositions using their own or classroom instruments, and body and found sounds. They can also add characters, such as a drum major and clowns, to the parade. The teacher might also couple this activity with a discussion of holidays or events which are typically commemorated with parades.

Drama & Music: Creative Activities for Young Children

9. NO!

Ask the children to use gestures, facial expressions and movements to interpret the characters and actions.

A stranger offers you a ride
The car looks comfortable inside
You know the rules of safety though
And you remember, "Just Say No!"

An older person touches you
And says to make it a secret
Remember "No!" and tell someone
When a secret's bad, don't keep it.

If you are offered beer or wine
Ask instead for milk or water
When you say "No!" to unsafe things
You're a wiser son or daughter.

10. NARRATIVE PANTOMIME STORY

Return to the noisy story, *Kayla's Present* (page 32) and play it as a narrative pantomime story, deleting character sounds and emphasizing actions.

Activities, Activities, Activities

QUIETING ACTIVITIES

Pantomime is generally used in quieting activities which are, as the name implies, ways of calming the children. Quieting activities are advised at the end of a session as a way to lessen the level of excitement and prepare children to move onto the next exercise or class. They can also be inserted between activities as a way to address pacing in a lesson. One energetic endeavor after another may produce too high a level of vigor among your children. By alternating these with quieting activities, a more reasonable classroom atmosphere can be maintained. Wait until all children are quiet before moving onto the next event as the calming value of these actions increases with time. Using a soft voice when presenting quieting activities also helps set the mood for playing. Try the following or create your own quieting activities.

You are a cloud gently floating across the sky.

You are singing on a music video and the person watching presses the pause button.

You are a spinning top that slows as it spins across the room and finally stops, coming to a rest on its side.

You are a flag fluttering in a stiff breeze and when the wind is calm, you droop.

Drama & Music: Creative Activities for Young Children

SEQUENCE GAMES

Order and organization can be vividly presented through sequence games. For this activity, the teacher prepares a set of index cards and randomly distributes the cards to the children. On one card the line, "You start the game" followed by an action appears. On all other cards, there should be a cue reading, "The person before you..." and an action for the new player to perform. Numerous topics and/or stories lend themselves well to this format. Children enjoy participating in games which have, for example, holidays, major episodes from stories, or recreational themes as their focus.

When devising sequence games, a few simple guidelines can be helpful. Word the cues using the same language as the action they describe. Also, by using different script, font, colored pencils, or some similar distinction, separate cues and actions on the card.

The person before you has come to the center of the room and pantomimed riding on a pony.
You come to the center of the room and pantomime feeding the chickens on the farm.

We recommend keeping a master list of the sequence of the cards for yourself, but do not number the cards given to the children. If an error is made and the sequence distorted, consider this a teaching opportunity and talk to the children about the importance of organizing ideas when communicating in oral, written, or physical form.

Several forms of reading are emphasized through sequence games. Children must silently read their cards in order to know what to do. They must "read" the nonverbal communication of others so that they can recognize cues. We also suggest ending the game by having each child read his or her card aloud and in order.

1. WAITING FOR THE SCHOOL BUS

You start the game. Come to the center of the room and pantomime putting on your new backpack.

The person before you has pantomimed putting on a new backpack.

You come to the center of the room and pantomime leaving your home, walking toward the bus stop and waving to your friends.

The person before you has pantomimed leaving home, walking toward the bus stop and waving to friends.

You come to the center of the room and pantomime taking off the backpack, climbing a tree, getting to a sturdy branch, and looking around to see if the bus is approaching.

The person before you has pantomimed taking off the backpack, climbing a tree, getting to a sturdy branch, and looking around to see if the bus is approaching.

You pantomime climbing down from the tree, putting on the backpack, and flexing your muscles to show strength.

The person before you has pantomimed climbing down from a tree, putting on a backpack, and flexing muscles to show strength.

You come to the center of the room and pantomime sitting on the sidewalk and giggling with your friends.

The person before you has pantomimed sitting on the sidewalk and giggling with friends.

You come to the center of the room and pantomime standing up when the bus arrives, boarding the bus, finding your seat, and sitting. Smile as you begin your trip to school.

2. SPECIAL DAYS SEQUENCE GAME

You start the game. Come to the center of the room and pretend to watch a football game on New Year's Day. Say, "Go team. Let's win!"

The person before you has come to the center of the room and pretended to watch a football game on New Year's Day. He or she said, "Go team. Let's win!"

You come to the center of the room and pretend that you are a groundhog on Groundhog's Day. Come out of your home, see your shadow, and go back inside.

The person before you has pretended to be a groundhog on Groundhog's Day. He or she has come out of his or her home, seen his or her shadow, and gone back inside.

You come to the center of the room and pretend to make a valentine and deliver it to a special friend.

The person before you has pretended to make a valentine and delivered it to a special friend.

You come to the center of the room and pretend to be a leprechaun. You say, "I found a four leaf clover and a pot of gold!"

The person before you has pretended to be a leprechaun and has said, "I found a four leaf clover and a pot of gold!"

You come to the center of the room and pretend to be a bunny delivering eggs and candy to children.

The person before you has pretended to be a bunny delivering eggs and candy to children.

You come to the center of the room and pretend to pick flowers and give the bouquet to your mother for Mother's Day.

The person before you has pretended to pick flowers and has given the bouquet to his or her mother for Mother's Day.

You come to the center of the room and recite the pledge of allegiance.

The person before you has come to the center of the room and recited the pledge of allegiance.

You come to the center of the room and say, "Ooh" and "Ah" as you pretend to watch fireworks.

The person before you has said, "Ooh" and "Ah" as he or she pretended to watch fireworks.

You come to the center of the room and pretend that you are swimming on a hot August day.

The person before you has pretended to be swimming on a hot August day.

You come to the center of the room, wipe your forehead and say, "That's hard work!"

The person before you has come to the center of the room, wiped his or her forehead and said, "That's hard work!"

You come to the center of the room and pretend to go from house to house saying, "Trick or treat" and holding out your bag for candy.

The person before you has pretended to go from house to house saying, "Trick or treat" and holding out his or her bag for candy.

You come to the center of the room and walk like a turkey in a circle saying, "Gobble, gobble!"

The person before you has come to the center of the room and walked like a turkey in a circle saying, "Gobble, gobble!"

You come to the center of the room and pretend to unwrap a present.

The person before you has pretended to unwrap a present.

You come to the center of the room and pretend to blow out the candles on a birthday cake.

The person before you has pretended to blow out the candles on a birthday cake.

You come to the center of the room and say, "Special days are fun!"

CIRCLE GAMES

The circle is an inviting configuration because of its inherent warmth and sense of equality. Children are often asked to sit or stand in a circle for creative drama games. These games often are used in developing ensemble play, which occurs when all children work together for the good of the exercise rather than for individual attention or merit. They also frequently test children's abilities in listening, concentrating, imagining, and speaking.

Regardless of the level of difficulty of the circle game you're leading, we encourage you to promote cooperation rather than competition. If during the game, for example, children are eliminated, they shouldn't be made to feel that they have "lost." If it suits your class and the exercise, consider allowing students to help those who might have difficulty remembering or contributing. If a lapse produces laughter, recognize its empathetic nature; children should be laughing with and not at each other. Thinking again about process, try to make all children feel like winners!

Drama & Music: Creative Activities for Young Children

1. A NEW MOTHER HUBBARD

The children should stand in a circle. The teacher states the first three lines of the rhyme and then calls on a child to continue. The child should not add lines of the rhyme as written, but should start to develop a new story for Mother Hubbard. When that child completes his or her contribution, another child should be selected to continue developing the new plot. As each new child is selected to add to the story, he or she should not repeat any previous words or pause for thinking time. If that happens, the child is asked to drop out of the game and another child is selected to continue the story. For example:

Teacher: Old Mother Hubbard
Went to the cupboard
To get her poor dog a bone...

Child #1:   She opened the cupboard door and looked inside.

Child #2:   Ah...Inside, she... *(Student is eliminated.)*

Child #3:   On the shelves, she found candy bars of rich chocolate and boxes and boxes of dog treats. Her dog barked with delight when he saw the food.

The game continues to be played in this fashion.

Activities, Activities, Activities

2. ELMER THE ELEPHANT

Children should be seated in a circle. The teacher begins by sharing the opening line of the story with the children. Then, moving around the circle, each child adds to the development of the plot. The children, however, must alternate contributions at your signal, changing the direction of the plot from positive adventures to negative ones and vice versa. For example:

Teacher: Elmer the Elephant was curious and loved to explore.

Child #1:   Today, he decided to explore the jungle. He began walking through the thick brush.

Child #2:   Suddenly, his foot became caught in something and he couldn't move. "Oh, no," thought Elmer.

Child #3:   Elmer struggled, but he couldn't free himself.

Teacher: Change.

Child #4:   Just then, Ms. Monkey came by and saw that Elmer was stuck. "You're caught in a hunter's net. I'll lift it so that you can move," she said.

The game continues in this manner.

Drama & Music: Creative Activities for Young Children

CHARACTERIZATION

Voice and body are used to create believable and interesting characterizations. Encourage the children to both look and sound like the characters they portray. Approach characterization work from both physical and vocal perspectives. Return to pantomime activities for review if desired before focusing upon vocal tasks.

1. WHO AM I PLAYING CARDS

This activity is designed to introduce young children to the legal system. Prior to playing the activity, students should research and report on the job responsibilities of people within the legal system. The teacher should prepare a set of cards. On each card, there should be a picture of a legal professional, such as a judge, attorney, or police officer. To play, each child draws a card and then is given thinking time to prepare an autobiographical introduction which is then shared orally. For the character portrayed, the child is to describe his or her responsibilities, but should not directly state who the person is. A truant officer, for example, might report as follows:

"I make sure that children go to school. It is my job to go to someone's home if that person has been absent without cause and to find out if there is a problem. I help children to stay in school."

The other members of the class then guess who the character is.

 ADDITIONAL IDEAS

• Ask the children to show how the characters on their cards move. An attorney, for example, might pace in front of a jury.
• Adapt this activity to explore careers associated with other fields.

JUDGE

LAWYER

POLICE OFFICER

IMPROVISATION IN MUSIC

To improvise is to invent freely and spontaneously. Improvisation is a highly creative act, however, those who improvise draw on a basic vocabulary. They just don't improvise out of a hat. You can develop each child's ability to improvise. First, you must help them acquire the vocabulary. Most of the rhythmic experiences, for example, with chants, nursery rhymes, listening games and rhythm instruments provide children with a storehouse of patterns that they can use when asked to "invent" something new.

Help children approach improvisation in a thoughtful matter. Many children will unconsciously spin out songs or chants as they play, jump rope, or engage in other activities. Others may need some guidance. Improvisations consist of the reorganization of musical rhythms or melodies. Encourage shy children to adapt familiar patterns from material they like when asked to improvise a new pattern.

The activities in this book gradually lead the child from very simple improvisatory work to more complicated work. Don't hesitate to use some of the simple experiences to "shore up" the children's skill and confidence levels. Children do need the opportunity to explore, practice and play with improvisation. When we ask a child to improvise, we are asking him or her to freely invent new material, i.e., to compose on the spot. Children may think improvising is a difficult task, and, in some respects, it is. It is not, however, reserved only for musical prodigies.

The second form of assistance you can provide for improvisation success is by structuring the activity. The environment for improvisation paradoxically needs some structure in which to be free. For example, if the improvisation involves inventing a rhythm pattern for the drum, you might encourage the children to think of a familiar pattern from a song and challenge them to make changes on it. In this way, you can launch the improvisation task by rearranging familiar patterns.

Melodic improvisations can be successful within a structured task, as well. The children might be encouraged to make up a new melody to the rhythm of a familiar song, such as *Are You Sleeping?*

We have found that improvisation activities are most likely to succeed if children are encouraged with short, small tasks within some structured parameters. Positive feedback, too, will go a long way in nurturing that creative spirit.

1. CALL AND RESPONSE

Call and response activities are natural ways to begin improvising with young children. Your "call" models pitches and rhythms, yet gives the children freedom to respond individually.

For warmups, sing each child's name and wait for an acknowledgement in return. To illustrate:

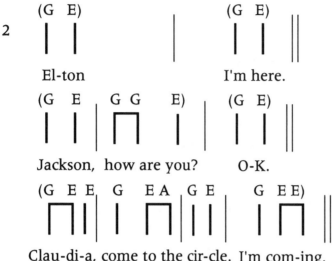

2. CHARLIE OVER THE WATER

(Music on following page)

Notice the form of this brief song. It is an echo song, but it has room for some individual improvisation. The first time through, it might be helpful to put together a "What Not Box" of assorted items. Allow each child to select an object from the box. (Such small items as a feather, paper clip, postage stamp and marble work well.) The object should be concealed from the rest of the group.

The teacher leads the song. When she arrives at the end of line two, she points to a child to get ready to lead line three and substitute the object.

After children are familiar with the format of the song and improvised line, they can imagine what Charlie caught without props. The teacher may wish to set categories of things for Charlie to catch. For example, the lesson might center on even numbers, vowels, four-legged animals, vegetables, etc.

CHARLEY OVER THE WATER

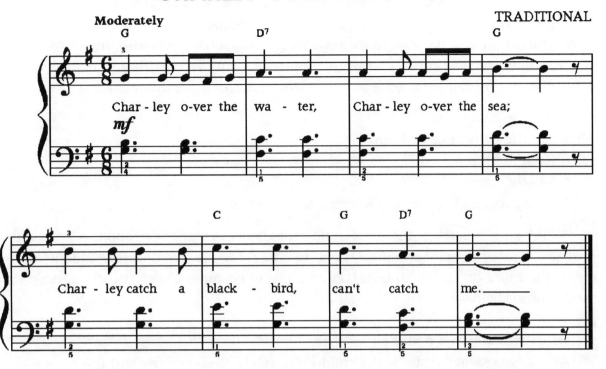

Char - ley o-ver the wa - ter, Char - ley o-ver the sea;

Char - ley catch a black - bird, can't catch me.____

Activities, Activities, Activities

IMPROVISATION IN DRAMA

Improvisation in drama also relies upon free invention and spontaneity within a basic structure. Here, scenes and stories emerge from a basic scenario. Improvisations are built upon "givens" or given information which correlates with dramatic elements. An improvisation can be developed using two or more of the following.

WHO: the characters
WHAT: the conflict or problem
WHERE: the setting
WHEN: the time
HOW: specifics of character interpretation or event

"Who" and "what" are the most important givens as stories are about people and conflicts. The one used least often is "how." The more information the students are given, the more precise the interpretation tends to become. Notice the difference in the scenarios below.

WHO: Two children and their teacher
WHAT: The teacher suspects the children have cheated on a test but the children maintain their innocence
WHERE: the classroom
WHEN: recess

WHO: A boy and girl, both in third grade; their teacher who is in her first year of teaching
WHAT: The teacher suspects the children have cheated on a test and wants the children to confess but lacks definite proof. The children maintain their innocence and want to avoid punishment.
WHERE: the classroom
WHEN: recess
HOW: The teacher is nervous and insecure; the students are defiant.

The "given" information is fundamentally the same in both examples, but the second scenario is more detailed and should produce a more structured interpretation. As you work with improvisations, you'll find that both types of scenarios are valid. The choice of how much information to give will depend upon whether you want to see how much the children can fill in from imagination or how precisely their interpretation can communicate certain characteristics.

Purists promote the spontaneity of improvisation and, after providing the scenario, ask players to begin without any planning time. This approach can be intimidating for young, inexperienced people and we suggest that *minimal* planning time be allotted. A careful line must be drawn here. Allow only enough planning so that children know the role they will play (who), how they will arrange the room (setting), and if there will be dialogue or if pantomime is to be used. You will have to carefully monitor here for, as soon as students begin to share such comments as, "I'll do this and then you say..." the planning has gone too far.

The open-ended nature of improvisations make them an excellent vehicle for repeated use. A scenario, for example, might be given to several pairs of players and each pair would develop a different story based upon their interpretation of the skeletal framework. Be aware, too, that improvisation is often an important first step in story creation. An idea might emerge during an improvisation that engages the interests and imaginations of the children and, through play, they will want to develop it. Using evaluation and replay for this purpose moves the material from improvisation to a more rehearsed piece of work. If the question arises, however, as to whether the resulting story is still improvisational, the answer may be that it no longer is but that it certainly began that way.

Improvisations may be humorous or serious in nature. Some teachers have enjoyed success with them in conjunction with stories, asking the children to improvise what they think happens next to the characters, changing the ending to a story through improvisation, fleshing out a scantily developed scene, or improvising to better understand how characters might feel.

Some children find improvisation difficult, especially in beginning work, and you may need to assist here. Consider intervention if the children can't think of anything to say or do, stare at each other, giggle, or take the story in a nonsensical direction. Should these difficulties arise, you might either stop the improvisation or enter as a character and, in role, try to bring the story back on track. In one class, for example, the teacher entered as a police officer when two children were having difficulty with an improvisation about a lost child at a carnival. By asking questions in role, the teacher was able to refocus the children who were then able to continue their story.

Numerous stories can result from the spontaneous expression of ideas in an improvisational format. So long as there are characters and conflict, students can explore, expand, and elaborate upon a minimal amount of given information.

1. IMAGINATIVE IMPROVISATIONS

Who: A babysitter and a small child
Where: The child's home
What: The babysitter wants the child to go to bed. The child wants to stay up late.

Who: A brother and a sister
Where: At their home
What: They want to give their mother a present but they don't have money to buy a gift.

Who: Two friends
Where: A carnival
What: Both want to ride a fast roller coaster but only one is tall enough to go on the ride.

Who: Two friends
Where: The zoo
What: One child loses a hat and wants to look for it, but the other child is afraid of the animals and wants to leave the zoo right away.
How: One child is timid and fearful; the other is daring and doesn't want to get into trouble for losing the hat.

2. PIONEER JOURNEY

Create three decks of cards, using either words, pictures, or both. One deck is the Character (Who) deck, one is the Motivation* deck, and the third is the Geography (Where) deck. Players select a card from each deck. They are then given thinking time and must create a story for the character and what happens to him or her in the geographical location. The story is to be shared orally with the rest of the class and told autobiographically.

Character cards might include the baseball player, the immigrant, the young child, the ballerina, the king, and the circus ringleader. Motivation cards might include to build a new house, to escape religious persecution, to start a new business, to have my own land, to make a new life for my young family, and to enjoy my summer vacation. Geography cards could include bodies of water, mountain ranges, plains, and deserts.

The activity can be replayed often simply by having children draw new cards and create new autobiographies each time.

Motivation is a part of characterization and relates to why a character behaves in a certain way or does a certain thing.

CHARACTER

Baseball Player

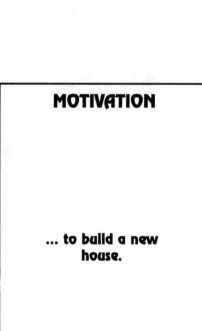

MOTIVATION

... to build a new house.

GEOGRAPHY

Amazon River

CHARACTER

Immigrant

CHARACTER

Young Child

CHARACTER

Ballerina

CHARACTER

King

CHARACTER

Circus Ringleader

Drama & Music: Creative Activities for Young Children

MOTIVATION		MOTIVATION
... to escape religious persecution.		... to start a new business.

	MOTIVATION	
	... to make a new life for my young family.	

MOTIVATION		MOTIVATION
... to have my own land.		... to enjoy my summer vacation.

GEOGRAPHY

Sahara Desert

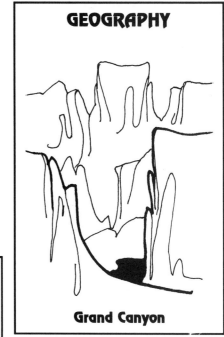

GEOGRAPHY

Grand Canyon

GEOGRAPHY

Himalaya Mountain Range

GEOGRAPHY

Deserted Island

GEOGRAPHY

North Pole

Drama & Music: Creative Activities for Young Children

STORY CREATION

Children enjoy making up stories and their delight increases if those same stories are dramatized. Story creation can be an independent activity or it can be the basis for story dramatization. A wide range of options is available to you and your students in this activity category.

Story creation can be conducted as a written activity and, in this approach, the children are encouraged to share orally what they have written with classmates. They can also enact the story they've written if desired. More commonly, however, stories are created orally or through dramatization. Additional plot and character development can be nurtured through replay. Sources for story ideas are limitless and include props, pictures, and songs.

Certain circle games and open-ended stories are popular vehicles deserving some special attention. In the former, the teacher usually begins by giving the opening of the story and having the children add to it. There is a certain security for children in going from one person to the next around the circle. In early playings, you are also likely to notice that contributions are brief. Children's entries tend to become longer as their confidence level builds.

There are variations, however, which challenge children and provide teaching opportunities related to language arts skills. You might, for example, wish to alter the rotational pattern. Children tend to be especially good listeners if they think they might be called upon next. A challenging variation is one in which a positive event or scene is alternated with a negative one. This also lends itself well to a discussion of plot development. Some teachers like to set limits, such as telling the children that they can't repeat the last few words of the person before them or that they must begin their portion within ten seconds of the previous person ceasing to speak. When these constraints produce humorous, nonsensical stories, use this to advantage and talk about story structure and how authors or storytellers organize elements for clear communication.

In open-ended stories, the beginning you provide may be as long or short as you like. More important than length is where the story breaks, even if this point is mid-sentence. A good open-ended story is one that has not been structured, consciously or unconsciously, to go in one particular direction. Instead, a successful open-ended story is one that you can use time and time again, or with several different groups of students, and see diverse results with each playing.

The teacher can call on each of the players who contribute or children can call on each other. In the latter strategy, a child would add as much as he or she wanted to the story and then call upon a classmate to continue. We suggest that when you play the open-ended story as a circle activity, you limit from three to five the number of players who add to the story. If too many add, the story might become illogical. You can always involve more children by beginning again and telling the new players to take the story in another direction. The last child in each group of three to five should conclude that story.

Open-ended story endings can also be dramatized. The children may wish to complete a story orally and then show the ideas through dramatization. Another strategy that we find works especially well is to give the opening to the children as they sit in a circle. You may need to repeat this more than once. Then, divide into groups and have each group create the rest of the story and share it though play. Using this technique involves group problem-solving and decision-making. Children, for example, must decide who will play the characters appearing in the opening and if others need to be added or deleted from what they have been given. They must decide if the story creation will involve dialogue. They must consider and establish setting. Often, the story ideas which emerge become the basis for further enhancement through story dramatization.

Drama & Music: Creative Activities for Young Children

1. THIS IS HOW MY STORY STARTS

Each child writes the opening line of a story. He or she then exchanges the opening line with a classmate. Each writes a story which starts with the line he or she has received. Completed stories are read aloud.

Children are then divided into small groups. Each group selects a story from those read. They rehearse and then perform the story for the rest of the class.

2. A NEW WAY TO GO TO SCHOOL

Divide the children into groups. Give each group a "transportation grab bag." Inside the bag, have pictures of three forms of transportation, such as a person walking, a bicycle, and a subway car. Transportation methods should vary for each bag. Tell each group that they are to imagine that they cannot get to school in the usual manner, but that they must create a story that tells how they get to school using the forms of transportation in their bag. All three forms must be included in the story. Stories can be shared orally or dramatized.

SUBWAY CAR

HELICOPTER

CAR

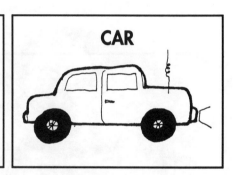

BOAT

PERSON WALKING

BUS

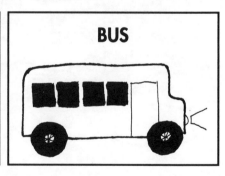

AIRPLANE

BICYCLE

SKATEBOARD

Activities, Activities, Activities

3. HELPING ON THE FARM

Children are seated in a circle. Each child adds to the story starter provided by the teacher with the stipulation that each new contributor mention an animal. The same animal can be mentioned more than once in the story. Children call on each other for additional content.

Story Starter: I help on the farm. Every morning I wake up early and go out to the barn. My first chore is to milk the cows.

 ADDITIONAL IDEA

•Change the location and create a new story. Children may help, for example, at the zoo or pet shop.

4. STORY CREATION FROM PROPS

Make grocery bags into grocery "grab bags" for story creation by filling them with newspaper ads, canned goods, cash register tape, play money, grocery list, coupons, meat label, etc. Group the children and give each group a bag containing at least three props. Have them create a story in which all three props must be used.

ACCOMPANIMENT

There are many ways to provide creative accompaniments to rhymes, chants, songs, movement, poems, stories, or recorded music. The key is to understand the function of the accompaniment.

One little story illustrates the role of the accompaniment clearly:

Mother asked Beverly to go to the store to buy a loaf of bread. When Johnny heard that Beverly was going, he asked Mother if he could go along. Mother said Johnny may **accompany** Beverly. Mother gave Beverly the money for the bread and told Beverly to be careful crossing the street. Beverly put Johnny in the stroller and walked to the store.

From the story, we help children realize the difference between the main figure and the accompaniment. Johnny is not an equal "partner" in this venture. We bring to the children's attention that only one person in this situation has the responsibility for the task. We ask, "Who is holding the money for the bread?" "Who is pushing the stroller?" "Who is watching for traffic when they cross the street?" "Who will select the loaf of bread?" "Who will count the change?"

Johnny just gets to "go along with" (as mother says, "accompany") Beverly in the story. He can enhance the trip or destroy it. He can hum and play with toys in his stroller, or he can scream and demand to get out of the stroller. Which type of accompaniment would you want?

After this discussion, it is easier to shape the role of the main "voice" in a musical piece and the minor "voice" which serves in the background. Those who accompany can make vital contributions to the performance if they remember their proper role.

We suggest numerous activities for accompaniments throughout the book. The creative use of body sounds, vocal sounds, found sounds and instrumental sounds will enchant the listener.

Accompany a variety of recorded music using different media. To get started, we suggest the following sequence:

1. Use a body sound, such as toe tapping, to keep the beat. Modify the volume of the tap according to the changes in the music.

2. Alternate body sounds. For example, stamp to the beat in loud portions of the music. Clap to the beat in moderate sections. Tip fingers to the beat during soft sections.

3. Add rhythm instruments for an accompaniment. Be selective in choosing appropriate instruments to accompany recordings, such as rhythm sticks to the beats of John Philip Sousa's marches.

Activities, Activities, Activities

1. RHYMES

Feel the beat of familiar rhymes. Most of them are felt in march-like patterns: *Jack and Jill*; *Humpty Dumpty*; *Little Bo Peep*; *Jack Be Nimble*; *Hey Diddle Diddle*; and *London Bridge*. Put together a classroom band of assorted rhythm instruments to support the recitation of familiar nursery rhymes. Because their voices are small, be sure the children do not play the instruments too loudly. An accompaniment should only support, not overpower, the important voice. Consider the following rhyme:

Little Miss Muffet sat on a tuffet,
Eating her curds and whey!
There came down a spider and
sat down beside her and
Frightened Miss Muffet away.

Various instruments can be used to keep the beat and provide additional expression to the perils of Miss Muffet. Consider using a combination of wood and metal instruments and increasing the number of instruments and their volume for special effects.

Drama & Music: Creative Activities for Young Children

CHORAL READING

Choral reading is typically reserved for middle school children. We believe, however, that primary children can recite literature as a chorus in an artistic manner if the work is at the appropriate interest level and length.

Every poem has rhythmic, lyric, and dramatic qualities that lend themselves to expressive reading. Even young children can recite a poem en mass in a meaningful manner. The teacher's role involves three responsibilities: (1) selecting an excellent piece of literature; (2) guiding the analysis for interpretation and "coloring;" and (3) conducting the actual reading.

As for proper selection of material, keep in mind that choral reading is enjoyable if the content relates to the children. Also, because the material must be memorized in order to watch the conductor, it needs to be relatively brief.

Below are some elements of music and characteristics of dramatic interpretation which can be applied as you analyze the reading's (in this case, a poem's) sound potential with the children. Obviously, the cognitive level of the child will determine how many of these elements should be explored in a given session.

RHYTHM/PHRASING

Does the poem's line have a beat to it?

Are the lines the same length?

Should we read the poem in a flowing, connected fashion until a punctuation mark?

Are there pauses before punctuation? If so, where?

Are there words to be accented or stressed?

Are there lines to be recited faster or slower than others?

What is the tempo or internal pacing of the poem? Does it change?

MELODY/VOCAL RANGE

Do the poem's lines have phrases?

Is there a contour or shape to the phrase, to suggest beginning with a lower voice, building to a high point, and ending with a lower voice?

Do any lines suggest upward or downward vocal direction (such as a question or words which imply upward motion)?

What choices should be made regarding inflection and articulation?

Does the timbre of the voices change as lines change and, if so, in what way?

HARMONY/CONCEPTUALIZATION

Should any parts of the poem involve two lines read at the same time?

Should any parts of the poem be echoed?

Should an ostinato be added at any point?

Should the poem or parts of it be accompanied by vocal sounds, body sounds, found sounds, or instruments?

Are sound effects appropriate?

Are there some lines which should be recited as solo readings? duo readings? small or whole group reading?

FORM/DRAMATIC STRUCTURE

How will the poem be introduced? How will the poet be announced?

Should all voices read throughout the poem?

Are there any parts which could be repeated for emphasis?

DYNAMICS

How loudly or softly should the poem be recited?

Do the dynamics change?

Beginning readers should nurture the skill of reading with expression. Take advantage of their reading abilities and combine the creative element of choral performance to achieve group interpretations of literature.

1. TRY IT THIS WAY

As an introduction to using the voice expressively in choral reading, have the children practice saying single words, phrases, or sentences in a variety of ways. Not only does this nurture vocal expressiveness, it also sharpens awareness of how sound and meaning go together in our spoken language. Look at the example which follows for suggested interpretations. Accented words appear in bold. For additional enjoyment, ask the children to create the list of words, phrases, or sentences to be practiced.

Ex. "I want to come with you."

C: **I** want to come with you!
C: I **want** to come with you.
C: I want to come. **With you.**

2. INTERPRETING POEMS

Select a poem from the children's reading assignments or from this book and invite students to perform each line two different ways. Encourage them to stress a word, change the speed, vary the volume, and so forth, for different creative effects.

ADDITIONAL IDEA

• See the poetry collections in Appendix B for appropriate poems.

LISTENING

Listening games sharpen children's aural skills in enjoyable ways. The activities in this section focus the child's attention on listening for sound characteristics. Then, they gradually expand the child's listening time span as well. Spend time each day with listening activities because they are directly related to language arts skills.

The beginning listener may not grasp all that is going on in the music during the first listening session. Sometimes the musical example is too long and other times too much is taking place in the music for the child to isolate something specific. Therefore, remember to keep the actual listening session brief. The music may be repeated often, but it should be of short yet intense duration to sustain the young listener's attention.

Drama & Music: Creative Activities for Young Children

1. SOUND IDENTIFICATION

Prepare a sampler cassette tape of various sounds of bells, buzzers, alarms and signals of household items such as the telephone, doorbell, microwave signal, computer beeps, alarm clock, fax machine, and so forth. Ask the children to listen very carefully to each sound and try to identify it. The important part of the discussion will be the aural clues they reveal that helped them come to their decision. Draw differences between the various sounds according to:

pitch level (highness or lowness);
volume (softness or loudness);
tempo (fastness or slowness);
duration (long or short);
pattern; or
any other characteristic they observed.

2. SONG IDENTIFICATION

Identify the familiar song in each experience by:

1. Humming the melody only.
   Ex.: Hum *Mary Had a Little Lamb.*

2. Clapping the rhythm only.
   Ex.: Play *Happy Birthday* on the rhythm sticks.

3. Singing only the first few notes of the song.
   Ex.: Using the syllable "loo," sing the first four notes of *Are You Sleeping?*

4. Listen to the following recordings and raise your hand when you hear the familiar song. Can you identify it by name?

Composition	Composer	Song
America	Ernest Bloch	*Pop, Goes the Weasel*
		Yankee Doodle
Children's March	Edwin F. Goldman	*The Farmer in the Dell*
		London Bridge
		Mary Had a Little Lamb
Death Valley Suite	Ferde Grofe	*Oh, Susannah*
Greeting Prelude	Igor Stravinsky	*Happy Birthday*
Symphony on a Hymn Tune	Virgil Thomson	*The Bear Went Over the Mountain*
Symphony #1		
Movement III	Gustav Mahler	*Are You Sleeping?*
Variations on "Ah", vous dirai-je Maman	Wolfgang Mozart	*Twinkle, Twinkle Little Star*

STORY DRAMATIZATION

Whether the material used for story dramatization is original or comes from a literary source, this type of creative drama activity tops the hierarchy of options for dramatic treatment. Story dramatizations afford the children an opportunity to explore worthwhile story material, analyze and understand dramatic action and conflict, investigate character relationships and plot developments, and empathize with characters. It brings together the skills that the children have built through earlier activities, such as characterization and dialogue creation. Casting here is individual, with one child per role, and story development is enhanced through replay and evaluation.

We offer several teaching tips here. Wait to introduce story dramatization until the children are ready for more complex activities and be certain to allow enough time for play. This is not a brief activity if you are really hoping to see in-depth characterization and plot development. Start with stories or poems that the children enjoy as this will increase their motivation to do well. Remember, too, that you don't have to play an entire story. Sometimes, the children may wish to work on only one scene. They may want to work on a little bit of the story each day for several days. They may wish to add, through improvisation or story creation, scenes that are not in the original piece. We encourage you to explore all options which you feel have validity for your class and curricular goals.

When guiding the children through a story dramatization, think in terms of dismantling and building to enrich and to enhance material. This process is one of working with small units of the story and then putting those units back together in a unified interpretation.

To begin, share the story with the children in a way that gains their interest. You may need to tell or review the story more than once. Children need to grasp important information, such as who the characters are, if they are to be successful in dramatizing. When you've finished presenting the story, it's a good idea to ask the children to repeat it to you in their own words. Then, discuss the specifics of the material with the group. What are the most important episodes? Why are these events important? Who are the major characters? Who are the minor characters? When you are satisfied that the children grasp the material, work with them to arrive at a consensus as to how many scenes there are, where each scene begins and ends, and what the main action or event is within each scene.

The children are now ready to begin "trying on" characters. This technique provides an opportunity for the children to play each of the major characters, even if they are not cast in the roles later in the dramatization. It also gives you opportunities to see if anyone is having difficulty imagining the characters and to preview some of their interpretive ideas. Identify the major characters in the first scene you wish to play. Select one. Ask the children to close their eyes and imagine that character. When they have a mental picture, ask them to raise their hands. When you can see that most or all of the children have ideas, ask them to open their eyes. Call on them to tell you one thing about the character as envisioned. Be certain to let them know that it's alright if they saw the same thing as a classmate or if their ideas are different. Typically, children will describe what the character is wearing or hair or eye color. Now, ask the children to show you, using pantomime, the character they envisioned engaged in some bit of action. It works well to allow the children to find personal space for this but to return to the circle or to their seats when finished so that you know when this segment has been completed. The action can be something found in the story or something that the character might typically do. You should repeat this process for each of the main characters in the scene.

Now, continue the "trying on" process in pairs or small groups and add dialogue. Again, allow the children to use personal space and then to return to their original places. Give them time to decide which of the main characters they will play. Unless it is required so that all children can participate, try not to double cast any roles here. The situation you present can come from the story or simply be something that these characters might do. Ask the children to think about possible dialogue. At the end of this segment, ask the children to describe what happened in the scene or what the characters said or did. Whenever possible, use open-ended questions to stimulate student thinking.

You are now ready to actually play the first scene. Review with the class where the scene starts and ends, the necessary action, the setting, and the characters. Cast by selecting players for roles or by asking for volunteers. Review ideas for dialogue and allow children to create a setting within the classroom if they so desire. The cast should now move into the playing space and other students should become audience members. Signal the start of the scene and begin play.

At the end of the scene, use evaluation to determine what went well and what could improve. We offer a word of advice here. Evaluation should encompass both strengths and weaknesses, although some children only want to talk about what was not good. Work towards a balanced critique that begins with the positive aspects of play. Talk about characters by their names, not by the names of the students playing the roles. Guide the children to articulate why they liked something, felt something could be done better or differently, or believed something was well done. It should be a goal to move beyond, "I did or didn't like it."

Initial playings tend to be superficial and depth of development relies upon replay and evaluation. Entertain suggestions for replay based upon incorporating new ideas, casting new players so that others have a chance to do a particular role, or including ideas for improvement. Play the scene again. Evaluate this playing. This pattern of evaluate, replay, evaluate should continue until the children are satisfied with the scene. Then, move onto the next scene.

The sequence of analysis, try-on, play, evaluation, replay continues for all of the scenes. These are then put together so that the entire story is brought to life through the emotional, verbal, physical, and active interpretative choices of the children.

1. FABLES

Fables are an excellent way to introduce young children to story dramatization. These short stories provide opportunities to explore dramatic action and character development. The simplicity of the plots facilitates dramatic interpretation. Children also enjoy discovering the moral of the story.

The Ant and the Grasshopper

One cool fall day, an ant was storing food for the winter. A hungry grasshopper asked the ant to give him something to eat. "What were you doing in the summer when I was busy finding this food?" the ant asked the grasshopper. "I was busy, too," replied the grasshopper. "I sang all day long." "Well," said the ant, "since you sang all summer you may dance all winter."
What is the moral?

Androcles and the Lion

Long ago, a slave named Androcles was running away. He was deep in the forest when he saw a lion moaning in pain. Although Androcles was afraid of the lion, he went to the animal to see what was wrong. The lion had a large thorn in his paw. Androcles pulled the thorn out and the lion felt much better.

Some time later, both Androcles and the lion were captured and taken to Rome. Neither knew of the other's plight. Androcles was sentenced to death. The lion was deprived of food for several days and was very hungry. The two met again when, as an amusement for the Emperor and his court, both were led into an arena where the lion was expected to attack.

The lion, however, remembered Androcles and was grateful to him for removing the thorn. He refused to attack. The Emperor was so impressed by this display of kindness that he freed them both.

Goldilocks and the Three Bears

As children become accustomed to story dramatization, they may wish to bring familiar stories to life. Simple stories that are known to the children, such as the classic which follows, are suggested.

Once upon a time there were three bears, Papa Bear, Mama Bear and Baby Bear. They lived in a house in the forest. One morning, the bears decided to take a walk in the woods while their breakfast porridge cooled. Off they went, leaving the door unlocked.

While they were gone, a young girl named Goldilocks came upon the bear's house. She looked inside and saw that nobody was home. "I'll just go in and look around," she said to herself, and she did. First, she saw the porridge and decided to taste it. She took a bite of Papa Bear's porridge, but it was too hot. Next, she tasted Mama Bear's porridge, but it was too cold. Then, she ate some of Baby Bear's porridge and it was just right! She ate all of the porridge.

She then saw chairs in the living room and decided to rest. First, she sat in Papa Bear's chair, but it was too hard. Next, she sat in Mama Bear's chair, but it was too soft. Then, she sat in Baby Bear's chair. It was just right! As she settled into the chair, it broke.

"I cannot rest on a chair," thought Goldilocks. "I'll see what's upstairs." On the upper floor of the house, she found three beds. First, she tried to climb into Papa Bear's bed, but it was too high at the head. Next, she tried Mama Bear's bed, but it was too high at the feet. Then, she climbed into Baby Bear's bed. It was just right and she fell into a sound sleep.

Soon, the bears came home. They saw the porridge. "Someone has been eating my porridge," said Papa Bear gruffly. "Someone has been eating my porridge," said Mama Bear sadly. "Someone has been eating my porridge," said Baby Bear, "and ate it all!"

Next, the bears went into the living room. "Someone has been sitting in my chair," said Papa Bear gruffly. "Someone has been sitting in my chair," said Mama Bear sadly. "Someone has been sitting in my chair," said Baby Bear, "and broke it!"

Papa, Mama, and Baby Bear went upstairs. Papa Bear looked at his bed. "Someone has been sleeping in my bed," Papa Bear said gruffly. Mama Bear looked at her bed. "Someone has been sleeping in my bed," Mama Bear said sadly. Baby Bear looked at his bed. "Someone has been sleeping in my bed," he exclaimed, "and there she is now!"

Goldilocks awakened and, upon seeing the bears, jumped out of bed. She saw an open window in the bedroom, climbed out, and ran away.

Activities, Activities, Activities

Anansi the Spider

The tales of Anansi are excellent for story dramatization. *Anansi the Spider*, by Gerald McDermott, relates one of Anansi's adventures in a form simple enough for children to appreciate and enact. The following summary previews the potential for simple characterizations and plot development in this version.

Anansi had six sons. Their names were See Trouble, Road Builder, River Drinker, Game Skinner, Stone Thrower, and Cushion. One day, Anansi went on a journey but he got lost. Each of his sons used his special skill to see that Anansi was rescued and that he returned home safely.

That night, Anansi found the moon in the forest and wished to give it as a gift. He asked Nyame, The God Of All Things, to hold the moon while he decided which of his sons was most deserving. Anansi's sons, however, fought over the gift so Nyame took the moon high up into the sky and there it remains.

Drama & Music: Creative Activities for Young Children

2. STORIES

When children dramatize stories, they utilize skills in characterization and directly experience dramatic elements such as plot, setting, theme and dialogue. They engage in an experiential and empathetic relationship with character and story. As casting is individual, each child is challenged to imaginatively, vividly and believably characterize and communicate the action and merits of the story.

The following lends itself well to a dramatization. This story has been freely adapted from a work by Hans Christian Andersen. The teacher may wish to cover new vocabulary words in this story with the children before undertaking a dramatization.

The Days of the Week

The days of the week wanted to get together to have a party, but they could not find a day when one of them was not busy working. To solve this problem, a day was added to February every fourth year. On this day, they have a costume party. The days of the week visit, eat and drink well, tell jokes, and have a good time!

On February 29th, Sunday, dressed all in black, is the first to arrive at the party. "I am the leader of the week and dress according to my station," Sunday says to the others as they arrive. "Sunday looks proper and pious," comment some of the days. "No," say the others, "Sunday is dressed for the theatre or a fancy ball." Sunday just listens and winks.

Monday is young and very energetic. He does not like to work nearly as much as he likes to enjoy himself. He likes to tell the others about the good times he has. "I love to dance. Whenever I hear music, I stop my work and go off to dance!" Monday dances around the room.

Tuesday is strong and comes to the party dressed as a police officer. "It is my job to make sure work rules are obeyed. I am the foreman of the factory. I am the boss at the office." The others are silent. "I'm joking," says Tuesday, but the others do not laugh.

Wednesday is very proud and announces to the others, "I am the most important day because I am the middle day. Three of you come before me and three of you follow me. You other days form an honor guard on both sides of me."

Thursday arrives at the party carrying a copper kettle and a hammer. "These are the symbols of my nobility," says Thursday, striking the kettle with the hammer. The others cover their ears because the noise is so loud!

Friday is usually a quiet young girl but at the party she is happy and carefree. "I have no work to do today," she proclaims brightly. "My work is done so let's have fun!"

Saturday stares at Friday. Saturday wears an old dress and carries a broom and bucket. "Work is never done," she grumbles. Saturday will not eat cake and ice cream with the others. "I prefer gruel," she says.

The days of the week all sit down at a long table. "To us!" toasts Sunday and the other days merrily reply, "To us!"

Activities, Activities, Activities

Furthering Your
Creative Potential

We hope the previous creative drama and music activities have whet your appetite for researching and developing additional ones. In this section, we have assembled ideas to extend your creativity as a facilitator of creative drama and music experiences. First, we offer some questions which may spark new ideas for you and inspire further creative lessons. These questions are followed by a discussion of formatting and combining creative activities within this book. The third portion provides you with planning structures to create original lessons. Please feel free to copy these plans for your files.

INSPIRING QUESTIONS

NAME GAMES

How can the children use their initials to learn vowels? consonants? alliteration? antonyms? synonyms?

Can name tags be "recycled" into bulletin boards? locker decorations? parent-teacher conference invitations?

FINGER PLAYS

What if children were to make finger puppets to dramatize finger plays? What materials are easiest to manipulate?

NURSERY RHYMES AND CHANTS

Using vocabulary or spelling words, how can the children create new chants that rhyme?

NOISY STORIES

What would happen if a noisy story used only body sounds? found sounds? rhythm instrument sounds?

What if you combined a name game, finger play, nursery rhyme and noisy story? If you rehearsed it well, could you share the performance with another class? Would you want the material to be thematically related?

SCAVENGER HUNTS

What would happen if the children played two or more cassette recordings of sounds simultaneously?

BODY SOUNDS

How will children explore different sounds from different positions? For example, will a stamping sound be different from a seated, kneeling or standing position?

VOCAL SOUNDS

Some vocal sounds make the throat vibrate. Others do not. How can the children tell the difference between the two types of sounds?

Could the class invite members of the elementary choir to sing for them?

FOUND SOUNDS

What if a list of all sounds were maintained that were found as a class? How many sounds could be found by the end of the year?

RHYTHM INSTRUMENT ACTIVITIES

There are many other types of instruments besides rhythm instruments. Do any of the children's relatives play instruments in bands? Could they come to school and show them the instruments and play them?

Could the class invite members of the elementary band or orchestra to play a concert for them?

SOUND JOURNALS

What colors are sounds? Why do some seem dark and some seem light? Would a crayon drawing tell something different than a painted drawing?

What if the children made a mural size sound journal? Could they show the "bigness" of sounds?

SONGS

What are the children's favorite songs? Why? How many songs can they sing by themselves?

Can they make up new songs? Can they put new words to a familiar melody?

CONCENTRATION GAMES

Most children can remember four or five sentences/items in concentration activities. What are some of the ways they can help each other remember more?

MUSICAL PUZZLES, QUESTIONS AND ANSWERS

Many times it is the teacher who asks questions during the school day. How many questions can they ask about music today?

MOVEMENT

As dancers, what type of dancers would they like to be? Can they dance a story? How would they "tell" the story without using words?

Can they understand a story from a ballet? a modern dance? a jazz piece?

Can the class invite relatives or members of a local dance troupe to teach basic jazz, tap or modern steps? Can they feel the difference?

What if they were to use scarves, ropes, or hoops in creative movement?

How do creative movement activities help them with characterization?

PANTOMIME

Have they ever met a mime artist? What parts of the body do they use?

How might masks be used to enhance pantomime?

Why is silence important in pantomime?

SEQUENCE GAMES

Can you think of an activity or story that has many parts to it? What if the children were to break it down into steps as a sequence game?

CIRCLE GAMES

Why do circle games use circles? What would a line game be like? Can they invent one?

IMPROVISATIONS

What are some ways the children can "save" things they've improvised? After they watch or listen to themselves improvise on video or cassette tape, are they proud of the creativity?

Invite members of a high school jazz band to perform for the children, particularly a performance which includes improvisation. How do jazz musicians improvise?

STORY CREATION

What are the children's favorite types of stories? Why do they like to listen to stories?

Can the class invite a storyteller to the classroom to share stories?

ACCOMPANIMENT

Can the class invite an accompanist to accompany songs? Why are the songs better with an accompaniment?

CHORAL READING

Does the class have a favorite poem? Would they like to arrange it for the class performance?

LISTENING

Do the children have a favorite piece of music? Would they like to share it with the class? How can you help them learn to like it more? What is special about the music?

STORY DRAMATIZATION

Does the class ever watch children dramatize stories on television? How do they act?

What if the class were to videotape one of their stories?

FORMATTING AND COMBINING ACTIVITIES

As you've read this book, you've had an opportunity to be introduced to many different types of creative drama and music activities. We hope that you found success with many of these with your children. To create full lessons, you may wish to juxtapose and combine activities to develop a topic from different creative angles.

You have, no doubt, noticed that some activities seem well suited to a particular topic and that by joining several of these together you can develop creative results. Let's say, for instance, that your class is studying animals. You might link the following activities for a creative session with beginning primary students:

> *Little Duck*
> *Five Little Monkeys*
> *You are a Duck*
> *Hickory, Dickory Dock*
> *Androcles and the Lion*

Another point of connection might be creative experiences associated with color, such as the activities below:

> *Mary Wore a Red Dress*
> *Sound Journals (in living color!)*
> *Colors*

You might combine the following sets for beginning and upper primary children all pertaining to time:

Kindergarten-First Grade Children	Second-Third Grade Children
Eight O'Clock	*Kayla's Present*
Hickory Dickory Dock	*Scavenger Hunt for Clock Sounds*
Kayla's Present	*What Time Is It?*

Or, another example might be days of the week. Experiences can be linked through the following combination:

> Adapting *Head and Shoulders* (page 15) to *Sunday, Monday*
> *Night and Day*
> *The Days of the Week*

We suggest that you review this book for exercises which seem to be related.

CREATING ORIGINAL LESSONS

Soon you will be writing your own activities. Begin, for example, to write activities for the following topics:

Transportation
The First Day of School
My Town
Favorite Stories
Special Occasions
The Last Day of School
Being a Friend
Win Some; Lose Some

Add to the following inventory pages. Begin by entering the activities used in this text. Continue the inventory to include your favorite finger plays, nursery rhymes, chants, and so forth with special care to note related content. Many times the title doesn't completely reveal the content. For example, *Baa Baa Black Sheep* may relate to a topic on animals, but it also may assist in reviewing topics on counting and numbers.

Then plan your lessons using the LESSON PLAN pages at the close of this section. You will be amazed how creative and resourceful you can be once you begin this process.

We wish you many rewarding experiences as you allow children to realize their creative selves.

NAME GAME INVENTORY

Title of Name Game Activity _____

Content Areas _____

_____

_____

_____

_____

_____

_____

_____

_____

_____

_____

FINGER PLAY INVENTORY

Title of Finger Play Activity _____

Content Areas _____

_____

_____

_____

_____

_____

_____

_____

_____

_____

_____

_____

NURSERY RHYMES AND CHANTS INVENTORY

Title of Rhyme or Chant Activity _____

Content Areas _____

_____

_____

_____

_____

_____

_____

_____

_____

_____

_____

NOISY STORIES INVENTORY

Title of Noisy Story Activity _____

Content Areas _____

_____

_____

_____

_____

_____

_____

_____

_____

_____

_____

_____

_____

SCAVENGER HUNT INVENTORY

Title of Scavenger Hunt Activity _____

Content Areas _____

_____

_____

_____

_____

_____

_____

_____

_____

_____

_____

_____

BODY SOUNDS INVENTORY

Title of Body Sound Activity _____

Content Areas _____

_____

_____

_____

_____

_____

_____

_____

_____

_____

_____

_____

VOCAL SOUNDS INVENTORY

Title of Vocal Sound Activity _____

Content Areas _____

_____

_____

_____

_____

_____

_____

_____

_____

_____

_____

_____

FOUND SOUND INVENTORY

Title of Found Sound Activity _____

Content Areas _____

_____

_____

_____

_____

_____

_____

_____

_____

_____

_____

_____

_____

ORCHESTRATIONS INVENTORY

Title of Orchestrations Activity _____

Content Areas _____

_____
_____
_____
_____
_____
_____
_____
_____
_____
_____

RHYTHM INSTRUMENT ACTIVITIES INVENTORY

Title of Rhythm Instrument Activity _____

Content Areas _____

_____
_____
_____
_____
_____
_____
_____
_____
_____
_____

Furthering Your Creative Potential

SOUND JOURNAL INVENTORY

Title of Sound Journal Activity _____

Content Areas _____

_____

_____

_____

_____

_____

_____

_____

_____

_____

_____

_____

_____

SONGS INVENTORY

Title of Songs Activity _____

Content Areas _____

_____

_____

_____

_____

_____

_____

_____

_____

_____

_____

_____

_____

CONCENTRATION GAMES INVENTORY

Title of Concentration Game Activity _____

Content Areas _____

_____

_____

_____

_____

_____

_____

_____

_____

_____

_____

MUSICAL PUZZLES, QUESTIONS AND ANSWERS INVENTORY

Title of Puzzle or Questions and Answers Activity

_____

Content Areas _____

_____

_____

_____

_____

_____

_____

_____

_____

_____

BODY SCULPTURES AND LIVING PICTURES INVENTORY

Title of Body Sculptures and Living Picture Activity _____

_____

Content Areas _____

_____

_____

_____

_____

_____

_____

_____

_____

_____

_____

_____

MOVEMENT INVENTORY

Title of Movement Activity _____

Content Areas _____

_____

_____

_____

_____

_____

_____

_____

_____

_____

_____

_____

CREATIVE MOVEMENT INVENTORY

Title of Creative Movement Activity _____

Content Areas _____

_____

_____

_____

_____

_____

_____

_____

_____

_____

_____

_____

PANTOMIME INVENTORY

Title of Pantomime Activity _____

Content Areas _____

_____

_____

_____

_____

_____

_____

_____

_____

_____

_____

_____

QUIETING ACTIVITIES INVENTORY

Title of Quieting Activity _____

Content Areas _____

_____

_____

_____

_____

_____

_____

_____

_____

_____

_____

SEQUENCE GAMES INVENTORY

Title of Sequence Game Activity _____

Content Areas _____

_____

_____

_____

_____

_____

_____

_____

_____

_____

_____

CIRCLE GAMES INVENTORY

Title of Circle Game Activity _____

Content Areas _____

_____

_____

_____

_____

_____

_____

_____

_____

_____

_____

_____

_____

CHARACTERIZATION INVENTORY

Title of Characterization Activity _____

Content Areas _____

_____

_____

_____

_____

_____

_____

_____

_____

_____

_____

_____

_____

Furthering Your Creative Potential

IMPROVISATION INVENTORY

Title of Improvisation Activity _____

Content Areas _____

_____

_____

_____

_____

_____

_____

_____

_____

_____

_____

_____

_____

STORY CREATION INVENTORY

Title of Story Creation Activity _____

Content Areas _____

_____

_____

_____

_____

_____

_____

_____

_____

_____

_____

_____

_____

Drama & Music Creative Activities for Young Children

ACCOMPANIMENT INVENTORY

Title of Accompaniment Activity _____

Content Areas _____

_____

_____

_____

_____

_____

_____

_____

_____

CHORAL READING INVENTORY

Title of Choral Reading Activity _____

Content Areas _____

_____

_____

_____

_____

_____

_____

_____

_____

_____

LISTENING INVENTORY

Title of Listening Activity _____

Content Areas _____

_____

_____

_____

_____

_____

_____

_____

_____

_____

_____

_____

STORY DRAMATIZATION INVENTORY

Title of Story Dramatization Activity _____

Content Areas _____

_____

_____

_____

_____

_____

_____

_____

_____

_____

_____

_____

_____

LESSON PLAN ——————————————————————————

Grade ———————————— Teacher ————————————
Topic ————————————————————————————————
———————————————————————————————————————

Activities to Use From This Book: ——————————————
———————————————————————————————————————
———————————————————————————————————————
———————————————————————————————————————
———————————————————————————————————————
———————————————————————————————————————

Activities I've Created: —————————————————————
———————————————————————————————————————
———————————————————————————————————————
———————————————————————————————————————
———————————————————————————————————————

LESSON PLAN ——————————————————————————

Grade ———————————— Teacher ————————————
Topic ————————————————————————————————
———————————————————————————————————————

Activities to Use From This Book: ——————————————
———————————————————————————————————————
———————————————————————————————————————
———————————————————————————————————————
———————————————————————————————————————
———————————————————————————————————————

Activities I've Created: —————————————————————
———————————————————————————————————————
———————————————————————————————————————
———————————————————————————————————————
———————————————————————————————————————

LESSON PLAN _____

Grade _____ Teacher _____
Topic _____

Activities to Use From This Book: _____
_____
_____
_____
_____
_____

Activities I've Created: _____
_____
_____
_____
_____

LESSON PLAN _____

Grade _____ Teacher _____
Topic _____

Activities to Use From This Book: _____
_____
_____
_____
_____

Activities I've Created: _____
_____
_____
_____
_____

Drama & Music Creative Activities for Young Children

Appendices

A. SUGGESTED STORIES

Aardema, Verna. *Why Mosquitoes Buzz in People's Ears*. New York: Dial Press, 1975.

Andersen, Hans Christian. *The Emperor's New Clothes*. Illustrated by Jack and Irene Delane. New York: Random House, Inc. 1971.

_____. *The Ugly Duckling*. Illustrated by Adrienne Adams. New York: Charles Scribner's Sons, 1965.

Atkinson, Mary. *Maria Teresa*. Durham, NC: Lollipop Power Books/Carolina Wren Press, 1990.

Brown, Marcia. *Stone Soup*. New York: Charles Scribner's Sons, 1947.

Commins, Elaine. *Lessons from Mother Goose*. Atlanta: Humanics Learning, 1989.

de Paola, Tommie. *Strega Nona*. New York: Prentice-Hall, 1975.

Dorros, Arthur. *Abuela*. New York: Dutton Children's Books, 1991.

Garcia, Maria. *The Adventures of Connie and Diego*. San Francisco: Children's Book Press, 1987.

Graham, Terry Lynne. *Fingerplays and Rhymes for Always and Sometimes*. Atlanta: Humanics Learning, 1984.

Greenfield, Eloise. *Nathaniel Talking*. New York: Black Butterfly Children's Books, 1988.

Grimm. *The Fisherman and His Wife*. Translated by Randall Jarrell. Illustrated by Margot Zemach. New York: Farrar, Straus & Giroux, Inc., 1980.

Hamilton, Virginia. *The People Could Fly*. New York: Alfred A. Knopf, 1985.

Haugaard, Erk Christian (trans.). *A Treasury of Hans Christian Andersen*. Garden City, New York: Nelson Doubleday, Inc., 1974.

Hume, Lotta Carswell. *Favorite Children's Stories From China and Tibet*. Rutland, Vermont: Charles E. Tuttle Co., 1966.

Kase, Robert, Ed. *Stories for Creative Acting*. New York: French, 1961.

Keats, Ezra Jack. *The Snowy Day*. New York: Viking, 1962.

Lattimore, Deborah Nourse. *The Dragon's Robe*. New York: Harper and Row Publishers, 1990.

Mitchell, Lucy Sprague. "Jump and Jiggle," in *Another Here and Now Storybook*. E.P. Dutton & Co., Inc., 1937.

Perrault, Charles. *Cinderella*. Translated and Illustrated by Marcia Brown. New York: Charles Scribner's Sons, 1954.

Polacco, Patricia. *Mrs. Katz and Tush*. New York: Bantam Books, 1992.

Potter, Beatrix. *The Tale of Peter Rabbit*. New York: Frederick Warne & Co., Inc., 1902.

Ross, Laura. *Puppet Shows - Using Poems and Stories*. New York: Lothrop, Lee and Shepard Co., 1970.

Sakai, Kimiko. *Sachiko Means Happiness*. San Francisco: Children's Book Press, 1990.

San Souci, Robert D. *The Talking Eggs*. New York: Dial Books for Young Readers, 1989.

Scheer, George F. *Cherokee Animal Tales*. New York: Holiday House, Inc., 1968.

Sendak, Maurice. *Where the Wild Things Are*. New York: Harper and Row, 1963.

Siks, Geraldine, Ed. *Children's Literature for Dramatization: An Anthology*. New York: Harper and Row, 1964.

Steig, William. *Dr. DeSoto*. New York: Farrar, Straus & Giroux, Inc., 1982.

Steptoe, John. *Mufaro's Beautiful Daughters*. New York: Lothrop, Lee & Shepard Books, 1987.

Tolstoy, Alexei. *The Great Big Enormous Turnip*. Illustrated by Helen Oxenbury. New York: Franklin Watts, Inc. 1968.

Tompert, Ann. *The Tzar's Bird*. New York: MacMillan Publishing Company, 1990.

Towle, Faith. *The Magic Cooking Pot*. Boston: Houghton Mifflin, 1975.

Viorst, Judith. *Alexander and the Terrible, Horrible, No Good, Very Bad Day*. Illustrated by Ray Cruz. New York: Antheneum Publishers, 1972.

Ward, Winifred, Ed. *Stories to Dramatize*. New Orleans: Anchorage Press, 1952.

White, Diane. *Can Mother Goose Come Down to Play?* Atlanta: Humanics Learning, 1990.

Williams, Vera B. *Cherries and Cherry Pits*. New York: Greenwillow Books, 1986.

Xiong, Blia. *Nine-in-One GRR! Grr!* San Francisco: Children's Book Press, 1989.

Yep, Laurence. *The Rainbow People*. New York: Harper and Row Publishers, 1989.

B. SUGGESTED POETRY COLLECTIONS

Bennett, Jill. *A Cup of Starshine*. San Diego: Harcourt Brace Jovanovich, 1991.

Bryan, Ashley. *Sing to the Sun*. New York: Harper Collins, 1992.

Cole, William. *A Zooful of Animals*. Illustrated by Lynn Munsinger. Boston: Houghton Mifflin Company, 1992.

Field, Rachel. *Poems*. New York: Macmillan Publishing Co., Inc., 1964.

Hall, Donald, Ed. *The Oxford Book of Children's Verse in America*. New York: Oxford University Press, 1985.

Hopkins, Lee Bennett. *Morning Noon and Nighttime, Too*. New York: Harper and Row, 1980.

Kennedy, Dorothy and X.J. *Talking Like the Rain - A First Book of Poems*. Illustrated by Jane Dyer. Boston: Little, Brown and Company, 1992.

McCord, David. *Away and Ago*. Boston: Little Brown & Co., 1974.

McCord, David. *One at a Time*. Boston: Little Brown & Co., 1986.

McCord, David. *Take Sky*. New York: Little Brown & Co., 1961.

Merriam, Eve. *Out Loud*. New York: Atheneum, 1973.

Merriam, Eve. *There Is No Rhyme for Silver*. New York: Atheneum, 1962.

Moore, John Travers. *Cinnamon Seed*. Boston: Houghton Mifflin Co., 1967.

Morrison, Lillian, Sel. *Rhythm Road - Poems To Move To*. New York: Lothrop, Lee and Shepard Books, 1988.

O'Neill, Mary L. *What Is That Sound!* New York: Atheneum, 1966.

Prelutsky, Jack, Sel. *Read-Aloud Rhymes for the Very Young*. Illustrated by Marc Brown. New York: Alfred A. Knopf, 1986.

Royds, Caroline, Sel. *Sing a Song of Popcorn*. Illustrated by nine Caldecott Medal illustrators. New York: Scholastic Inc., 1988.

Russo, Susan. *The Moon's the North Wind's Cooky*. New York: Lothrop, Lee and Shepard Co., 1979.

Silverstein, Shel. *A Light in the Attic*. New York: Harper and Row, 1974.

Silverstein, Shel. *Where the Sidewalk Ends*. New York: Harper Collins Publishers, 1974.

Thomas, Marlo. *Free to Be...You and Me*. New York: McGraw-Hill, 1974.

Wilner, Isabel, Sel. *The Poetry Troupe - An Anthology of Poems to Read Aloud*. New York: Charles Scribner's Sons, 1977.

C. MUSIC RESOURCES

INSTRUMENT COMPANIES

General Music Store
19880 State Line Road
South Bend, IN 46637

LMI
127 N. Walnut St.
Itasca, IL 60143
1-800-456-2334

Music is Elementary
P.O. Box 261030
Cleveland, OH 44124
1-800-888-7502

Suzuki Musical Instrument Corporation
P.O. Box 24263
San Diego, CA 92196-9877
1-800-854-1594

RECORDINGS, BOOKS, MUSIC, AND VIDEOS

Classroom Music Resources
Belwin Inc.
15800 N.W. 48th Avenue
Miami, Fl 33014

High/Scope Press
Educational Research Foundation
600 N. River Street
Ypsilanti, MI 48198-2898
313-485-2000

The Music Book
Holt, Rinehart and Winston
383 Madison Avenue
New York, NY 10017

Music Educators National Conference
1806 Robert Fulton Drive
Reston, VA 22091
1-800-828-0229

Silver Burdett Music: Early Childhood
Silver Burdett Co.
250 James St.
Morriston, NJ 07632

The Spectrum of Music with Related Arts: Kindergarten
Macmillan Publishing Co., Inc.
866 Third Avenue
New York, NY 10022

Wardbrodt
2200 W. Beltline Hwy.
P.O. Box 526
Madison, WI 53701
1-800-722-7760

Anderson, William and Patricia Shehan Campbell, Eds. *Multicultural Perspectives in Music Education*. Reston, VA: MENC, 1989.

Andress, Barbara. *Music Experiences in Early Childhood*. New York: Holt, Rinehart and Winston, 1980.

Arnett, Hazel. *I Hear America Singing!* New York: Praeger Publishers, 1975.

Barlow, Betty M. *Do It Yourself Songs*. Delaware Gap, PA: Shawnee Press, 1964.

Glass, Paul. *Songs and Stories of North American Indians*. New York; Grosset and Dunlap, 1968.

Glover, Joanna and Stephen Ward, Eds. *Teaching Music in the Primary School*. New York: Cassell, 1993.

Hackett, Patricia. *The Melody Book*. Englewood Cliffs, NJ: Prentice-Hall, Inc., 1983.

Hart, Jane, comp. *Singing Bee - A Collection of Favorite Children's Songs*. Illustrated by Anita Lobel. New York: Lothrop, Lee & Shepard Books, 1982.

Lawrence, Marjorie. *What? Me Teach Music?: A Classroom Teacher's Guide to Music in Early Childhood*. Sherman Oaks, CA: Alfred Publishing Co., 1982.

McLaughlin, Robert and Lucille Wood. *The Small Singer*. Glendale, CA: Bowmar Publishing, 1969.

Paz, Elena. *Arroz Con Leche*. Popular Songs and Rhymes from Latin America. New York: Scholastic, Inc., 1989.

Yolen, Jane, Ed. *The Lap-Time Song and Play Book*. Musical arrangements by Adam Stemple. Illustrated by Margot Tomes. San Diego: Harcourt Brace Jovanovich, Publishers, 1989.

HICKORY, DICKORY, DOCK

Brightly

MOTHER GOOSE

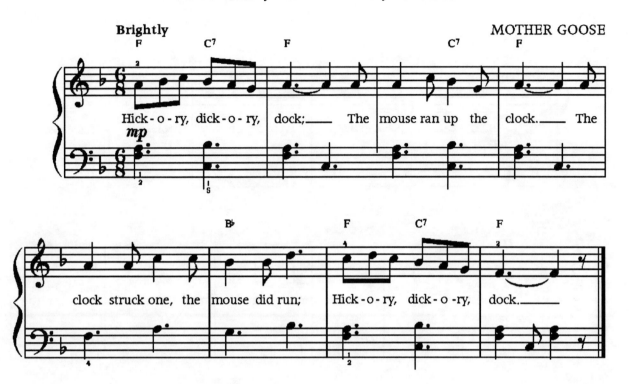

Hick - o - ry, dick - o - ry, dock;___ The mouse ran up the clock.___ The

clock struck one, the mouse did run; Hick - o - ry, dick - o - ry, dock.___

ACTIVITIES
Nursery Rhymes and Chants – 1. Hickory Dickory Dock
(page 27)

BAA, BAA, BLACK SHEEP

MOTHER GOOSE

ACTIVITIES

Rhythm Instrument Activities – 2. Classroom Instrument Bands
(page 45)

LOVE SOMEBODY
(Yes, I Do)

TRADITIONAL

2. Love somebody, can't guess who!
Love somebody, can't guess who!
Love somebody, can't guess who!
Love somebody, but I won't tell who.

3. Love somebody, yes I do!
Love somebody, yes I do!
Love somebody, could be you!
Love somebody, loves me too!

ACTIVITIES

Rhythm Instrument Activities – 2. Classroom Instrument Bands
(page 45)

MERRILY WE ROLL ALONG

Moderately

ENGLISH FOLK SONG

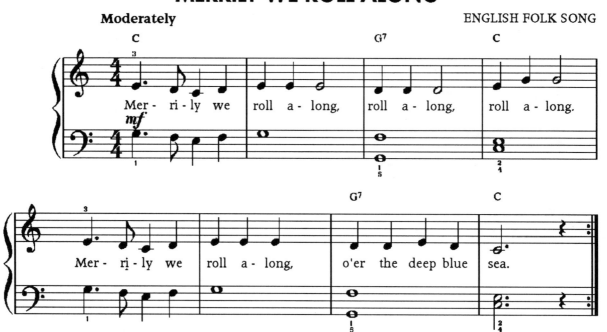

ACTIVITIES
Rhythm Instrument Activities – 2. Classroom Instrument Bands
(page 45)

LITTLE JACK HORNER

Moderately bright

MOTHER GOOSE

Lit - tle Jack Hor - ner sat in a cor - ner, Eat - ing his Christ - mas pie. ___ He put in his thumb and pulled out a plum, And said, "What a good boy am I." ___

ACTIVITIES

Rhythm Instrument Activities – 2. Classroom Instrument Bands
(page 45)

LOOBY LOO

Joyfully

ENGLISH TRADITIONAL SINGING GAME

Here we go loo-by loo. Here we go loo-by light,
Here we go loo-by loo. All on a Sat-ur-day night. I
put my right hand in, I put my right hand out, I
give my right hand a shake,shake,shake, And turn my-self a-bout.

Chorus
Verse: I put my left hand, etc.
Chorus
Verse: I put my right foot in, etc.

Chorus
Verse: I put my left foot, etc.
Chorus
Verse: I put my whole self in, etc.

ACTIVITIES

Rhythm Instrument Activities – 2. Classroom Instrument Bands
(page 45)

ROW, ROW, ROW YOUR BOAT

TRADITIONAL ROUND

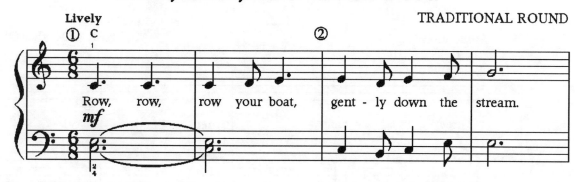

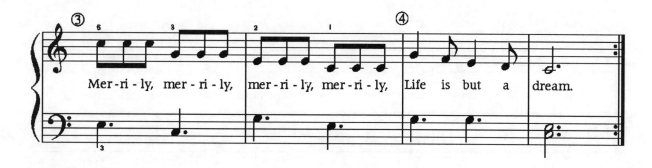

ACTIVITIES
Rhythm Instrument Activities – 2. Classroom Instrument Bands
(page 45)

THREE BLIND MICE

Moderately   MOTHER GOOSE ROUND

ACTIVITIES
Rhythm Instrument Activities – 2. Classroom Instrument Bands
(page 45)

Drama & Music Creative Activities for Young Children

HUSH, LITTLE BABY

Moderately

G   D⁷   TRADITIONAL

1. Hush, lit-tle ba - by, don't say a word; Ma-ma's goin' to buy you a mock-ing-bird. If that mock-ing-bird don't sing, Ma-ma's goin' to buy you a dia-mond ring.

2. If that diamond ring turns brass,
   Mama's goin' to buy you a looking glass.
   If that looking glass gets broke,
   Mama's goin' to buy you a billy goat.

3. If that billy goat won't pull,
   Mama's goin' to buy you a cart and bull.
   If that cart and bull turn over,
   Mama's goin' to buy you a dog named Rover.

4. If that dog named Rover won't bark,
   Mama's goin' to buy you a horse and a cart.
   If that horse and cart fall down,
   You'll still bethe sweetest little baby in town.

ACTIVITIES

Rhythm Instrument Activities – 3. Song to Story
(page 45)

BLUE BIRD

Briskly

AMERICAN SINGING GAME

Blue-bird, blue-bird, Through my win-dow, Blue-bird, blue-bird.

Through my win-dow, Blue-bird, blue-bird, Through my win-dow,

Oh, John-ny, I am tir-ed.

Take a little girl, tap her on the shoulder,
Take a little girl, tap her on the shoulder,
Take a little girl, tap her on the shoulder,
Oh, Johnny, I am tired.

ACTIVITIES
Songs – Other Surefire Songs
(page 57)

THE FARMER IN THE DELL

Moderately

TRADITIONAL

2. The farmer takes a wife, etc.
3. The wife takes a child, etc.
4. The child takes a nurse, etc.
5. The nurse takes a dog, etc.

6. The dog takes a cat, etc.
7. Teh cat takes a rat, etc.
8. The rat takes the cheese, etc.
9. The cheese stands alone, etc.

ACTIVITIES

Songs – Other Surefire Songs
(page 57)

RING AROUND THE ROSY

Moderately

TRADITIONAL

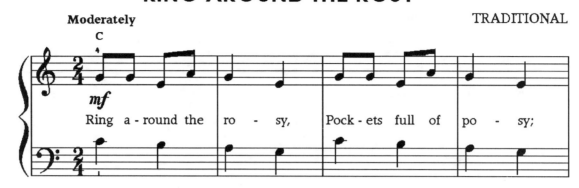

ACTIVITIES
Songs – Other Surefire Songs
(page 57)

RAIN, RAIN

UNIVERSAL FOLK MELODY

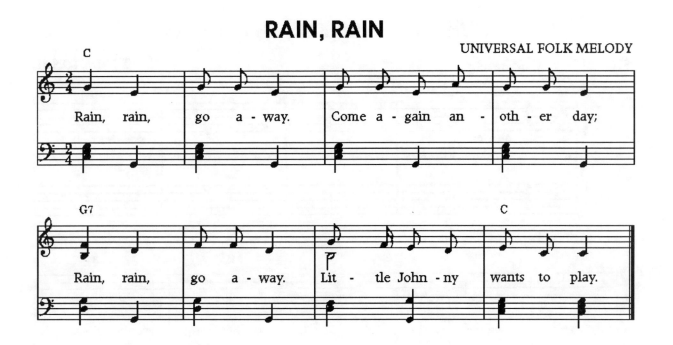

ACTIVITIES

Songs – Other Surefire Songs
(page 57)

TWINKLE, TWINKLE, LITTLE STAR

ACTIVITIES
Rhythm Instrument Activities – 3. Song to Story
(page 45)

Songs – Other Surefire Songs
(page 57)

BYE, BABY BUNTING

MOTHER GOOSE

ACTIVITIES
Songs – Other Surefire Songs
(page 57)

HOT CROSS BUNS

MOTHER GOOSE

ACTIVITIES
Songs – Other Surefire Songs
(page 57)

SALLY GO 'ROUND THE MOON

TRADITIONAL

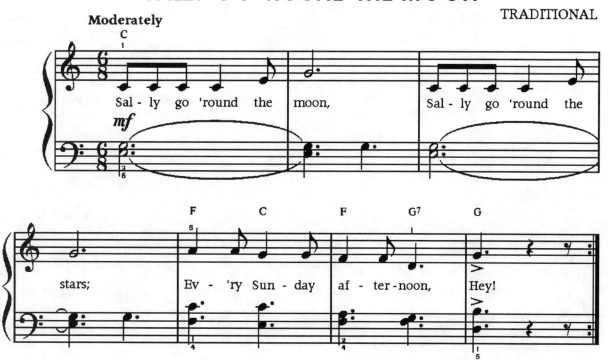

ACTIVITIES

Songs – Other Surefire Songs
(page 57)

THIS OLD MAN

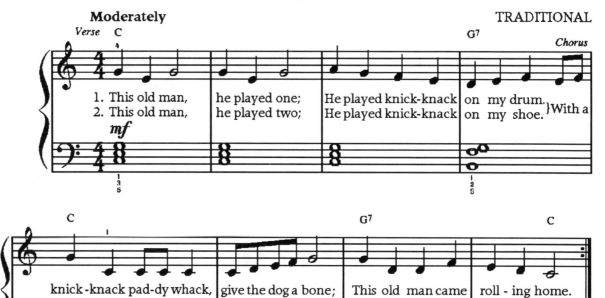

3. This old man, he played three,
   He played knick-knack on my knee. (Chorus)

4. This old man, he played four,
   He played knick-knack on my door. (Chorus)

5. This old man, he played five,
   He played knick-knack on my hive. (Chorus)

6. This old man, he played six,
   He played knick-knack on my sticks. (Chorus)

7. This old man, he played seven,
   He played knick-knack up to heaven. (Chorus)

8. This old man, he played eight,
   He played knick-knack at the gate. (Chorus)

9. This old man, he played nine,
   He played knick-knack on my line. (Chorus)

10. This old man, he played ten,
    He played knick-knack over again. (Chorus)

ACTIVITIES
Songs – Other Surefire Songs
(page 57)